GREAT SPORTING FIASCOS

Sebastian Coe, Bill Beaumont, Frank Bruno,
Eddie Edwards, Duncan Goodhew, David Gower,
Gary Lineker, Tessa Sanderson, David Wilkie,
Ian Woosnam and friends present...

GREAT SPORTING FIASCOS

FOREWORD BY
HRH THE DUKE OF EDINBURGH KG KT

President of the National Playing Fields
Association

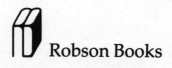

Robson Books

First published in Great Britain in 1991 by Robson Books Ltd,
Bolsover House, 5-6 Clipstone Street, London W1P 7EB

Edited by Tony Brett Young

British Library Cataloguing in Publication Data
  Great sporting fiascos.
  I. Title
  796.0207

ISBN 0 86051 768 3

Typeset by Bookworm Typesetting, Manchester
Printed in Great Britain by Butler & Tanner, Frome and London.

Acknowledgements

Our thanks go to the following individuals who have helped enormously in putting this book together: Helen Hays, Bill Lothian, David Lloyd, Michael Meech and Kevin Taylor. Grateful thanks also go to Matthew Engel and Frank Keating for permission to use pieces which originally appeared in the *Guardian*, and to Martin Johnson for his piece which originally appeared in the *Independent*. Also, thanks to Den, Paul Johnson, Larry, McTrusty, Mahood, David Myers and Roy Nixon for their splendid cartoons.

The Derby –
Philip chatting to
the winning
jockey

Sport can be a very serious business. For some it is a way of making a living, while for others it is desperately important to win. The trouble is that most sport is performed with other competitors and in front of spectators. Opportunities for embarrassing moments are therefore always present. If the sport happens to involve horses, the chances of being humiliated are even greater.

To be laughed at for some silly mistake is bound to be a bit trying at the time, but sooner or later most true sportsmen - and sportswomen - come to see the funny side of it and before long they are dining out on the story.

"Great Sporting Fiascos" has been produced in aid of the National Playing Fields Association's "Action for Play" appeal. It is the latest in a number of books whose royalties have gone to the NPFA. The last one raised enough money to buy land for ten football pitches. All those who have contributed to this book realise, probably better than most, just how important it is for young people to be able to enjoy play and recreational facilities. The NPFA exists to protect existing facilities and to create new ones where the need is most urgent.

1991

Peter Alliss has had a long career in golf, initially as a top-class player, and later as a commentator and writer. The height of his playing career came in 1958 when he won the Italian, Spanish and Portuguese Opens in three successive weeks. Today he is perhaps the best-known golfing commentator on television in both Britain and the United States.

LUND IN HOT WATER

It has been said many times before that golfers do some extraordinary things. This was brought home to me a number of years ago when I was watching the Italian Open golf championship being played on the spectacular Pevero golf course which comes under the domain of the Aga Khan and is situated on the north-eastern side of Sardinia.

Pevero was designed by the great American architect Robert Trent Jones. As I looked at the incredible job he had done in creating the course, I marvelled at his audacity in suggesting to the Aga Khan that he could build a course there. I also marvelled at HRH's budget. But then I suppose his subjects might have given him his weight in rubies and pearls two or three times that year.

My story begins at the twelfth hole. A relatively innocuous looking pond, it would be wrong to call it a lake, nestles on the left hand side of the green. It is perched on one of the many boulders that border the fairway (the course was built virtually on top of, and through, a small mountain range). I watched through a pair of modest binoculars the approaching match.

One was the unmistakable figure of Henrik Lund, a fine young man from Denmark, who loved the game of golf but, in all honesty, was never going to make it to the top of the professional ranks. Running a club, looking after the members, and being an all-round jolly good egg - yes. But his playing ability was only about four out of ten. Nevertheless, a great trier.

Henrik was always immaculate but on this occasion, due to circumstances beyond his control, he was unable to afford a caddie so was carrying his own clubs. He struck his second shot with a 3-iron, but it just turned a little right to left, the breeze caught it and swept it into the dreaded pond. A big splash went up and Henrik moved forward with a purposeful stride.

He got to the edge of the pond and looked and, lo and behold, there almost within reach was a golf ball. Well, he *thought* he could reach it. He must have been running out of ammunition because he could have gone back behind the hazard, keeping the point where the ball last crossed the line into the water between him and the hole, pitched up on the green, dropped a couple of strokes, and moved on.

But no. Henrik didn't like that idea, or he might have been short of golf balls. He reached in, and just couldn't make it. One of his partners came over, held his hand, and he stretched even further. But - you guessed it - suddenly a slip on the bank and into the water went Henrik! The water was about five feet deep, and he rose like Excalibur from the lake, shook himself, and pulled out the golf ball. However, ignominy piled upon ignominy – after all that it wasn't his ball!

He went on, wet through, and not smiling too often, to complete the round in 89 shots. Golfers, you see, are strange creatures, and what was going through Henrik's mind as he disappeared beneath the surface of the pond will stay only with him for the rest of his days.

FEELING THEIR WAY

In 1908, the England-Wales rugby match was played at Bristol in thick fog. Reports of the match tell how every time a player scored, one of the team cautiously made his way to the side of the pitch to tell the press – and the crowd.

The Argentinian, **Ossie Ardiles**, was one of his country's outstanding footballers, playing in the team which won the World Cup in 1978 on his home soil. In 1978 he joined Tottenham Hotspur to become one of their most successful foreign signings. He became Manager of Swindon Town in 1989 and then Manager of Newcastle United in 1991. He has earned a reputation as one of the most popular and respected overseas players ever to be involved in the game in England.

THE GREAT ENGLISH GAME

In 1980, Tottenham were playing Middlesborough who had a foreign player, a Yugoslav whose name I can't remember. In our team we had a player called Terry Yorath who was not exactly famous for his football skills.

In one incident, he kicked the Yugoslav into the air. It was a bad foul, but not particularly violent. The Yugoslav went to the floor, and stayed there for ages complaining to the referee about the behaviour, or misbehaviour, of Terry Yorath.

It was somewhat over the top, and the referee was becoming very agitated about his performance and the fact that he did not stand up and get on with the game. I happened to be in the vicinity of the incident, and approached the referee, and said sympathetically to him: 'Bloody foreigners!'

GETTING HIS BIG BREAK

The French rugby player, Jean-Pierre Salut, was carried off injured before he even reached the pitch in the France-Scotland match at the Stade Colombus in Paris in 1969. As he was running up the stairs from the dressing room, Salut tripped – and broke his ankle.

Another French rugby player was even less fortunate in his international career. Gaston Vareilles was selected to play for his country against Scotland in 1911. The team was travelling to the match by train when Vareilles wandered off during a brief stop to buy himself a sandwich. Unfortunately, he was delayed, and returned to see the train disappearing into the distance. He missed the match, and was not chosen to play for his country again.

Dave Bassett has been Manager of Sheffield United Football Club since 1988. As a player he represented teams in the former Athenian and Southern Leagues, including Wimbledon before it was promoted to the League. He then became Manager of Wimbledon and took the club from the fourth to the first division. Dave then had a brief spell as Manager of Watford before joining Sheffield United, initially helping the team to avoid relegation, and then to gain promotion to the first division.

SILENCE IS GOLDEN

A couple of years ago, I had a 'slight altercation' with a Football League referee after he had, in my opinion, made a series of diabolical decisions against my team. For reasons of decorum and propriety – and to avoid the charge of 'bringing the game into disrepute' – I shall not mention the referee's name.

Throughout the course of that particular season, the BBC had been filming at Bramall Lane to prepare a six-part documentary series entitled *United*. Its purpose was to look behind the scenes at a professional football club and to record the happenings in considerable detail – warts and all. They filmed in the dressing room before and after matches; in the Directors' Room at a board meeting; in the homes of the players – and so on. I'd become so accustomed to the almost continuous presence of the cameras that I started to forget they were there, and began to ignore them.

A few days after my slanging match with the referee, we had a social function at Bramall Lane, and quite unexpectedly I was asked to say a few words. Because I had no prepared speech, I stood up and said the first thing that came into my head – which happened to be about that referee and his incomprehensible decisions. So, simply for the sake of a cheap laugh from the players and supporters in the audience, I called the referee a very rude name – a name of which Mary Whitehouse certainly would not have approved. The audience laughed, I got a good round of applause at the end of the speech, and I sat down feeling well pleased with myself.

Unfortunately, I was completely oblivious to the fact that the BBC had filmed the whole thing! Imagine my horror therefore when, a few months later, as I was watching *United* on television – it was an episode sub-titled 'The Manager' featuring the work of yours truly – I was suddenly confronted with a close-up of myself making that speech, including that word. How are the mighty fallen! My self-satisfaction with the speech turned dramatically into embarrassment.

It all got me into awful trouble with the football authorities and, though I wrote a letter of apology to the referee concerned, I don't think that he, or the powers-that-be, have yet forgiven my indiscretion.

Looking back it now seems quite funny, but it certainly wasn't funny at the time. 'Walls have ears,' they say. It's equally appropriate to say that television has eyes and ears – and I shall never forget that salutary lesson. But I can't promise never to make the same type of mistake again!

DEBITS AND CREDITS

The World Football Club Championships of 1967 involved Celtic, who represented Europe, and the Argentinian team Racing Club, the South American champions. Celtic won the first leg at Parkhead 1-0, but Racing made it all-square with a 2-1 win at home.

The deciding match, played in Montevideo, was an ill-tempered affair and six players were sent off – four from Celtic and two from Racing. With the odds very much in their favour, Racing went on to win the match 1-0.

Each of the Racing players was presented with £2,000 and a new car, but for the Celtic players there was no such reward – they were each fined £250 by their club.

'. . . AND IT LOOKS AS THOUGH HUTCHINS IS
OPERATING IN MIDFIELD THIS WEEK . . .'

MISSING THE BOAT

A Brigadier-General Critchley was as keen an amateur golfer as he was a professional soldier. In 1937, he entered the Amateur Golf Championship at Sandwich in Kent, but shortly before the event, he was required to travel to New York. He planned his return so that he would still be able to compete, but did not allow for the fog which delayed the return of his ship to Southampton. When finally it docked, he had just a few hours to make it to Sandwich, nearly 150 miles away.

Undaunted, the General rang the organizers and told them he was on his way. He then arranged to charter an aircraft to fly him to the championship venue. As time ticked by, and the moment he was due to tee off approached, the aircraft at last swooped down over the course. The soldier-golfer ordered the pilot to dip the plane's wings to tell the officials he had arrived. It then landed in a nearby field, and Critchley grabbed his clubs and ran to the first tee. However, he was six minutes late, and was disqualified.

Dave Beasant will be remembered as the first goalkeeper to save a penalty in an FA Cup final at Wembley when he captained Wimbledon's winning side in 1988. After ten years with Wimbledon, he transferred to Newcastle United for a season before moving to Chelsea. Dave has won seven England 'B' caps and has represented his country twice in full internationals.

GOAL SNEAK

W hen I was a Wimbledon player, in the fourth division, we were playing away at Hartlepool (not the most picturesque ground in the world) on a wet, muddy Saturday afternoon.

Unfortunately, objects often get thrown at the opposing goalkeeper during matches, and this happened to me on this occasion - the object was an unopened Mars bar. It missed, landing just beside me. I picked it up, gestured my thanks to the fans behind the goal, put the Mars bar into my glove bag, and carried on with the game.

A short time later I was on the edge of my penalty box when there was an outbreak of cheering and laughter from behind. I looked round and

saw a young boy in the back of the goal net, looking through my glove bag to reclaim his Mars bar!
When he found it he held it up like a trophy, and
leapt back over the barrier into the cowd. When I
looked later, I found that he'd left my goalkeeping
gloves worth about £60 in the bag.

I wonder, was that young boy a certain Paul
Gascoigne? He certainly had a liking for Mars
bars.

A RIGHT ROYAL DISASTER

In 1908, when the modern Olympic
Games were held in London for the first
time, the marathon event was run
between the royal residence at Windsor
Castle and the White City stadium in west
London. The distance was standardized at
26 miles 385 yards, with the extra yards
added on so the competitors would finish
right in front of Edward VII's royal box. The
additional distance proved disastrous for
an Italian competitor, Dorando Pietri, who
collapsed from exhaustion after entering
the stadium and was within sight of the
finishing line. Well-meaning officials
rushed to his aid, and helped him finish
the race – but he was subsequently disqualified as a result.

Bill Beaumont won thirty-four Rugby Union caps for England, twenty-one of them as captain, during an outstanding career in the late seventies and early eighties. He also played seven matches for the British Lions. Following his retirement on medical advice he has established a highly successful career as a businessman, commentator and television personality.

A NEW ZEALAND TOUR IS NO HONEYMOON

I was selected as a British Lions standby for the 1977 tour of New Zealand, and was asked to fly out at short notice as a replacement when one of the touring party was injured. However, my tour didn't get off to the best of starts.

I had already booked a holiday with my wife Hilary in Minorca as a belated honeymoon, but had to cancel that (after a reassuring chat with Hilary). I then tried to recover the cost of the cancelled holiday, but the travel company pointed out that I would have to produce a medical certificate declaring I was unfit to travel. That little masquerade would have appeared somewhat suspect if the patient simultaneously managed to win a Test place for the Lions in the middle Saturday of the Minorca holiday!

I broached the subject of costs with the secretary of the British Lions and he pointed out that I was meant to be a standby all summer; it was my own fault for trying to fit in a honeymoon before the end of the Lions tour.

On 10 June, I headed for Heathrow Airport, accompanied by John Lawrence, secretary of the Four Home Unions. As we approached Heathrow, traffic ground to a standstill because of a crash on the M4. To catch the flight, we had to abandon the car and run the last two miles. John set off in front clutching his umbrella, and I pounded along behind with a bag in each hand.

Nonetheless, he steadily opened up a commanding gap and, considering he was in his fifties, a huge question mark appeared against my state of health and fitness. I arrived in the nick of time to catch my flight, and collapsed in my seat, dripping with sweat and absolutely knackered.

I had a journey of a mere thirty-two hours in which to recover.

GIVEN THE BIRD

The cricketer with the worst record in the history of the English county competition was A. H. S. Clark who played for Somerset in 1929. Following his selection for the county side, he scored nine successive ducks. He was then dropped to bring his unfortunate first-class career to an end.

> ⓜ
>
> **Dickie Bird** is perhaps the best-known cricket umpire in the world, and has stood in more than 120 Tests, World Cup matches and one-day internationals, including the Centenary Test Match between England and Australia in 1980. Before becoming an umpire, Dickie Bird played county cricket for Yorkshire, the county of his birth, and for Leicestershire. In 1986 was made an MBE for his services to cricket.

CAUGHT SHORT IN THE MIDDLE

When you are out in the middle as an umpire, so many funny things happen. I remember umpiring a Test Match at Old Trafford when the Australian Bob Holland was bowling from my end to Graham Gooch. Graham hit a full toss straight at me like a bullet. It hit me on the ankle, and down I went.

On to the field came the Australian physio to give me treatment. It was a full house at Old Trafford that day, and I didn't get a lot of sympathy from them, but there was a tremendous roar for the physio when he came on. After I had received treatment, Bob Holland, the bowler, thanked me for saving four runs. However Graham Gooch was not very happy because he had lost four runs.

On another occasion during a Test Match – again at Old Trafford, and this time England *v* West Indies – I urgently wanted to use the toilet so I stopped the match and said to the players: 'I am very sorry gentlemen, but nature calls.' The players were very amused as I ran off, and there was a tremendous roar from the crowd. They obviously knew where I was going!

It's amazing what can happen in the middle of a Test Match.

Dickie Bird also tells the story of losing the famous white caps he sometimes wears to umpire:
Before a West Indies series starts I always have to have a box of white caps sent from the firm who make them because the West Indies pinch my white caps just like shelling peas. They just pinch them off my head. As I come off the field they just whip them, and I have to have a box sent.

There's one story – perfectly true. I was umpiring a County Championship match at Lord's and I didn't have my car so I travelled by train from the north of England, and I caught a London bus from King's Cross to my hotel in Hyde Park. A London bus, and this big West Indian conductor came round: 'Fares please . . . fares please,' and I looked at him and he had this white cap on.

So I said: 'Excuse me, Sir, where did you get that white cap?'

'This white cap, man? Why, haven't you heard of Mister Dickie Bird?'

'I'll say this for Fred Higgins he's got Exquisite manners . . .'

REFEREE ON THE SCORE SHEET

Actions by the referee can have a crucial effect on the result of any football match, and the man in black is sometimes blamed – fairly or unfairly – by players or spectators for the loss of a particular game. In a third division match between Plymouth Argyle and Barrow in 1968, however, there is no doubt that the referee Ivan Robinson cost Plymouth the match – he scored the only goal.

With just over ten minutes to go, the score was still 0-0 when Barrow, the home side, were awarded a corner kick. The ball was cleared, but Barrow player George McLean took a wild shot at goal from outside the penalty area. The ball was always going wide, but towards the referee who was standing about a dozen yards from goal. He leapt to avoid the ball, but too late and it struck his foot, rebounded past the stranded keeper, and into the goal.

The rules make it clear that the ball is still in play if it rebounds off the referee or the linesmen if they are on the field of play, and Robinson had no alternative but to award the goal, to the delight of the Barrow team. George McLean was subsequently credited with the goal, perhaps to save the referee's blushes.

In spite of Plymouth's frantic efforts to retrieve the game, Barrow hung on to win by the single goal. For Plymouth – and probably for the referee – it was a particularly long journey home that night.

⚽

Trevor Brooking is one of football's most respected personalities. He made more than 500 league appearances for West Ham, and was capped forty-seven times for England. He is now a successful businessman, a BBC broadcaster, football coach and is involved in sports administration.

FOR BROOKING READ BRUNO

Most sports players have their embarrassing moments. One of my worst was when I was a young player for West Ham and had been in the side for just a few months. About mid-way through the first half in one match, we received a throw-in. If you are a mid-field player as I was, you quite often receive possession from your thrower. So I began to walk away from the throw-in area to relax my marker to make him think I wasn't interested in receiving the ball. My tactics were to quickly turn and run back to the space I'd created, and actually take the throw.

Unfortunately for the referee he decided just then he was in a dangerous area and began to run past me from behind to get out of the area of play.

I didn't see him, and at that moment began to twist around. As I turned my elbow caught his temple and he just collapsed in a heap. Of course most of the players were stunned and just stood there, but the West Ham captain, an old fellow called Bobby Moore, ran up and picked up his whistle which was lying on the ground and blew it to stop play. The physiotherapist and linesmen ran on, but the referee was still concussed and unable to continue, and had to be helped from the field.

So I suppose I am one of the few players who have actually knocked out a referee during a match and been allowed to stay on the field. Afterwards, after he'd recovered, I saw his wife who had come to watch him referee the game. We had a little chuckle because she said: 'I've been wanting to do that to him for years, so you've saved me the trouble.'

THROWN BY THE QUESTION

Bill Toomey, the USA's 1968 Olympic decathlon champion, had one of his most stunning encounters with a feature writer from one of America's biggest newspapers.

'How far can you actually throw the decathlon?' she enquired.

GAVASKAR'S GO-SLOW

Limited overs cricket matches have become an accepted part of the cricket scene, in spite of criticism by the purists and traditionalists. The skills needed to play the game are substantially different from those of three-, four- or five-day cricket, and an ability to pace an innings is essential. With experience, many top cricketers have become expert at judging when to accelerate their batting, or how to bowl tightly to restrict scoring. In the first World Cup competition played in England in 1975, one of the world's great batsmen got it completely wrong.

The match, between England and India, was played at Lord's, and England won the toss and batted. From the start of the innings, the home batsmen scored at the rate of more than five runs an over. A dashing innings of 137 from Dennis Amiss, 68 by Keith Fletcher and 51 not out by Chris Old contributed to an astonishing 334-6 in 60 overs.

However, when it was India's turn to bat, they appeared to make no attempt to chase the big England total. Opener Sunil Gavaskar, one of the best batsmen his country has produced, was the chief culprit. He batted throughout the 60 overs for just 36 runs.

The crowd was frustrated by the go-slow, and at one stage, police and ground officials had trouble keeping spectators off the pitch. A policeman was injured when he was punched by one irate spectator. Even the Indian captain was unable to persuade Gavaskar to get a move on. At the end of their tortuous innings, India still had seven wickets in hand, but had fallen short of their target by a staggering 203 runs.

Frank Bruno became boxing's European heavyweight champion in 1985, and has lost only three fights in an illustrious career, including a world title bout against the fearsome Mike Tyson. In addition, Frank has become involved in a range of activities, even pantomime

THE WIENER SCHNITZEL BY A KNOCKOUT

I always try to be super-fit for my fights but, fortunately, being a heavyweight I've never had to worry about getting down to a certain weight to qualify for my division. I also like my food, so I feel a bit sorry for boxers who have to starve themselves.

I once read about a lightweight called A. Hamilton-Brown who had that problem. He took part in the 1936 Olympics in Berlin, but had a lot of trouble making the weight to qualify, and tipped the scales just on the limit for his first fight. He must have wondered whether it was all worthwhile when he was beaten on a split decision in the opening bout, even though he thought he had done enough to win.

He was very disappointed – and hungry – so he went out on the town for a good meal. It was only then that one of the judges discovered he had awarded his points to Hamilton-Brown's opponent, a Chilean, by mistake. By the time the team manager found Hamilton-Brown, he had already tucked into a substantial German menu, and you know what they're like.

He spent the rest of the evening and next morning trying to shed weight again, but when he stepped on the scales for his next bout, he was still five pounds too heavy and had to be disqualified.

THE BEAR FACTS

Magistrates in South Shields, Tyne and Wear, heard a strange case of sabotage recently when a teenager appeared before them following an incident at a greyhound meeting in Sunderland.

The defendant was alleged to have thrown a teddy bear in front of the greyhounds at the Northern Puppy Derby. The court heard how the dogs had given up the chase for the electronic hare, and leapt on the teddy bear to try to savage it. The race was declared void.

The youth needed a police escort to leave the track because of threats from angry punters. When he appeared in court he was fined £100. The magistrates also agreed to a request from the prosecution for the teddy to be confiscated.

David Bryant won his first bowls championship – the Clevedon club handicap – in 1948 when he was sixteen. Since then, he has won twenty-six English titles, the world outdoor and indoor singles championships three times each, and the Commonwealth singles title four times. He has twice been decorated by the Queen for services to bowls, gaining the MBE in 1969 and the CBE in 1980.

THE END WAS IN SIGHT

It was enough to make a bowls commentator blush when Minehead Bowls Club celebrated the opening of two new indoor rinks.

I was delighted to be invited, along with my long-time bowls partner and BBC commentator, David Rhys Jones, to unveil a plaque in the West Somerset club's smart new social area.

But the focus of attention soon turned to an unscripted unveiling of a rather different kind.

Towards the end of the scheduled exhibition match, and heralded by a horrible, fateful, unmusical kind of 'zzrrippffkk' sound, David's breeches rent embarrassingly asunder. The end, indeed, was in sight.

Swiftly to the rescue came England team captain

Reproduced by courtesy of the *Bristol Evening Post*

Johnny Wiseman, of Donyatt, nimbly covering David's cheeky accident with his England cardigan, like a policeman preserving a streaker's modesty.

The bottom line, if I may put it that way, belonged to Minehead Chairman Norman Ackland, who thanked the visitors for giving such a wonderful exhibition.

Never has David been in more dire need of heeding the bowler's motto: 'Always play defensively – and never leave your end exposed.'

MISTAKEN IDENTITY

World motor racing champion Ayrton Senna is maybe not as well known as he might think.

Dispatched to obtain a photo file of Senna by a sub-editor in a leading Scottish newspaper a copy boy duly returned from the library clutching a collection of pictures of ... Ayr Town Centre.

Andy Cameron's Sunday radio show, *Andy Cameron's Sunday Joint* has become something of an institution in Scotland. He has also presented his own television series for both BBC and Scottish Television, and has been awarded both the television and radio 'Personality of the Year' awards presented by the Scottish radio industries and the *Daily Record*. A keen golfer, he plays regularly in pro-am tournaments throughout the country helping to raise money for a variety of charities.

TAXI DRIVER

In 1985, Sandy Lyle won the British Open at Royal St Georges in Kent. A month later, I played with him and two other partners at Haggs Castle in Glasgow in a pro-am match. You can imagine that with his Glaswegian connection (both his parents come from the city), there would be a big turnout to watch the new champion. I reckon there were 3,000 people around the first tee.

Sandy hit the ball further than I usually go on holiday. Then, some wag in the crowd shouted out: 'Go on, Andy, get it past his!'

I was searching for a suitable funny reply when another voice piped up: 'You'll have to put it in a bloody taxi to get it past that!'

PUNCTURE STOPPED PLAY

Wimbledon 1991 was probably one of the wettest on record with rain interrupting play on most days of the tournament. But not all of the stoppages were due to the weather.

A long rally was in progress during a doubles match on Court 2 when a loud explosion echoed round the stands. There was immediate concern among players and spectators and thoughts of a possible terrorist attack at the All England Club.

The answer soon became obvious however when it was seen that the tall umpire's chair had developed a Pisa-like list. One of its four tyres, designed to help easy removal, had burst and left the umpire leaning precariously.

The serious business of tennis was forgotten temporarily until the puncture was repaired, and the umpire's dignity – and balance – was restored.

Gina Campbell is the daughter of Donald Campbell, the only person to set new land and water world speed records in one year. He was killed attempting to push the world water speed record beyond 300 mph on Coniston Water in 1967. In 1984 Gina won her class in the UK Off-Shore Boating Association Championships, and went on to win the European title for her class of powerboat the following year. In October 1984, she became the fastest woman on water when she set a new women's world water speed record of 122.85 mph at the National Water Centre in Nottingham. In 1990, she increased this to 146.475 mph on Lake Karapiro in New Zealand.

ALL AT SEA

One of my most hair-raising – and amusing – memories is the Round Britain Powerboat Race in 1984. We set off from Portsmouth on a July day with a force seven gale in prospect. Of the forty boats which set out, only fifteen reached Falmouth, which was the destination on the first day. And my boat *Bluebird*, my colleague and I arrived on a trailer!

We had fought our way through the most frightening seas I have ever encountered between the Isle of Wight and Weymouth, but one of our engines failed and we had to pull into a sailing club.

There was no one there to repair the engine. But the rules of the race said as long as you made an effort to get to the day's destination you could continue the race, though with so many penalty points that you had no hope of winning.

From the *Yellow Pages* I traced a man who advertised trailer hire, and he came to the rescue. The snag was that his trailer was not large enough to take *Bluebird*. However, he said he had noticed a much larger trailer which had been chained to a post not far away for several weeks, and he thought the unknown owner would not mind if we 'borrowed' it. To make a comic situation complete, he chained his much smaller trailer to the post in place of the one we had borrowed.

There was a thirty foot sea as we rounded Land's End on the way to Fishguard next day. The troughs between the waves were so deep that the Coastguard did not even log that we had passed!

We were taking in so much water that it upset the electrics. Before long, everything – switches, steering wheel, gear level – was live. By the time we were off Newquay, the bilge pump was not working and we had to pull in.

There was no alternative but to stay there the night. We had nothing with us, apart from my Access card and as we walked up the High Street to a supermarket to buy some clothes I was in hysterics. The fear and tension as we rounded Land's End had put bodily functions beyond our control, and my partner had admitted to me at the time that he had peed in his wet-suit. As we walked through Newquay it was coming down his legs and his white socks were slowly turning yellow!

To say that the rest of the race was less hazardous or less amusing would be an underestimate. But I remember well that by the time we were coming south along the Yorkshire coast, fatigue was taking over and we had not kept an eye on our charts or landmarks as conscientiously as we should have.

Having lost our bearings we were relieved to see a couple of men fishing from a boat. We switched off our engines and cruised up behind them. 'Excuse me, can you tell me where we are?' I shouted. We must have approached them more quietly than we imagined. Both of them jumped as though they had seen a ghost. What they saw must have seemed even stranger – a flashy race boat in smart colours decked with race numbers and Union Jacks, and a couple of southerners in posh wet-suits and bright scarlet helmets having to admit they were lost.

'Scarborough, luv,' one of them replied as they recovered. We thanked them and went on our way as though we had just paused in a country lane to ask directions. But there we were, three miles off the coast in the North Sea. And they just turned and continued fishing.

MAN'S BEST FRIEND

Ally MacLeod, the former Scotland football manager, is now enjoying relative tranquillity in charge of Queen of the South where he perhaps occasionally reflects on one of his darkest moments.

Scotland had just drawn 1-1 with Iran in the 1978 World Cup Finals and a solitary MacLeod was sitting gathering his thoughts when a small dog approached. 'Ah, my only friend in the world,' he remarked. The dog then bit him.

HIT AND SPIT

Two Italian footballers playing in the Canadian National League were disciplined in 1972 for spitting at the referee. One was suspended for eighteen months, the other for four years. A League official explained that the stiffer sentence was because 'one spit missed, the other spit hit'.

Menzies Campbell was captain of the UK athletics team in 1965 and 1966, and was the Amateur Athletics Association's 220 yards champion in 1964 and 1967. He held the UK 100 metres record from 1967-74, and competed in the Olympic Games in 1964 and the Commonwealth Games in 1966. Today, Menzies Campbell is a barrister and MP for Fife North East. He has been a member of the UK Sports Council and the Scottish Sports Council, and is the Liberal Democrat spokesman on sport.

QUICK OFF THE MARK

My story is about two incidents which occurred a week apart, and they both involved myself and a very fine, and rather cavalier, sprinter of my vintage called David Jones. He was a wonderful man, one of the famous Jones boys. One weekend, Great Britain had a dual meeting against Hungary and I was running the third leg of the 4 x 100 metres relay, and David Jones was running the fourth.

As I tore round the bend of the old White City Stadium (now of course the site of the BBC),

David Jones took off yards ahead of the mark. As a result I never got near him, and we failed to transfer the baton. Afterwards when we were being brought to book by the team manager, David Jones said – with total insouciance: 'Quite simple. Incoming runner was fading, and couldn't keep up the pace. Incoming runner couldn't catch me.'

Just one week later, we were competing in the European Cup final in Germany. On this occasion David Jones was running second, and I was running third. He came charging down on his leg, and I took off when he hit the mark. I ran out of the box, and he didn't catch me. The team manager took us aside once more to ask what the hell had happened. This time David Jones's response – in the same tone of voice – was: 'Quite simple. Outgoing runner went off far too fast.'

OPEN GATE

In a London Friendly League fixture between a Millbank XI and Battersea Park FC in February 1991, three backpasses to the Battersea goalkeeper ended up as own-goals in the first fifteen minutes. Battersea eventually lost the match 7-4. Their goalkeeper's name? Simon Gatehouse.

Will Carling, the Harlequins and England centre, was chosen to captain the national rugby side in only his second international match, against Australia in 1988. He led the England team in its grand slam win in the 1991 Five Nations championship – its first for a decade.

NO SHOW FOR SLOCOCK

One of my favourite stories about Rugby concerns a player called Arnold Alcock who turned out regularly for his club just after the turn of the century. He was a keen but fairly undistinguished player, even at that level.

One day in 1906, he received a letter inviting him to play for England against South Africa. He was, of course, very proud to be chosen to represent his country, and must have thought that all of his efforts had finally been rewarded.

It was only when he reported for the game that it was discovered that the invitation letter should have been sent to another player, Andrew Slocock. It was then too late to switch the two men, and Alcock went on to represent his country in the match, perhaps one of the luckiest players ever to do so.

I just hope that Willie Carson never takes up Rugby – he might end up captaining England by mistake.

AIR FORCE CRASH

Australian Rules Football is notable for its high scoring, and on occasions that can result in big wins – and heavy defeats. In October 1978, the *Melbourne Age* news-paper reported on two matches played by teams representing the Royal Australian Air Force in a local competition:

'The RAAF had a bad day in the North Gippsland Football League yesterday. Their first 18 was defeated 192 points to one, while the seconds lost by 196 to one.'

Willie Carson rode his first winner at Catterick in 1962 and went on to become champion jockey in 1972. Since then, he has failed just once to ride 100 or more winners in a season – and then only because he was injured. He has a total of fifteen Classics to his credit, including three Derby winners. Willie has been described as the Queen Mother's favourite jockey and, in 1990, he brought home his 3,112th winner to take him to third place as Britain's most successful jockey behind Lester Piggott and Sir Gordon Richards.

THE PONTEFRACT GHOST

It was a sunny day at Pontefract. The late afternoon sun beamed over the course, and I was happily out front, having made all the running.

I was on the rails, and turned into the straight, a furlong and a half from home. To my surprise I thought I could hear something coming up behind me. I turned round and saw a shadow tucked in behind. 'Right,' I thought, 'we'll get rid of him.'

I gave my horse a backhander, and asked him for more effort. Again I glanced round, still it was there.

Jesus, I couldn't get rid of it. He's going to beat me! So I gave my horse everything. We zoomed the last few yards, and to my intense relief were first past the post.

Now I had time for a real look round. Nothing there! I'd spent a furlong and a half racing my own shadow, and we'd won by fifteen lengths!

TAKING THEIR TIME

The great English jockey, Sir Gordon Richards, was an outstanding judge of the pace of a horse. But he also listened closely to trainers' instructions.

At Birmingham in August 1949, he was booked to ride Ridge Wood in the Midland St Leger Trial Stakes over thirteen furlongs. The trainer, Noel Murless, made it clear to Richards that he should not take the lead. Unfortunately, Dick Perryman, the trainer of Courier, the only other horse in the race, had given exactly the same instructions to his jockey, Tommy Lowrey!

When the event started, neither horse moved. Courier turned round in the opposite direction, and it appeared to spectators that there had been a false start. The starter called out to the two jockeys to begin racing, and then sent his assistant over to crack the whip.

At last, Courier and Ridge Wood broke into a slow canter, with both jockeys keeping them under tight reign. These methods were not at all popular with racegoers, and they began to jeer the two men who took little notice. They went on to cover the first furlong at snail's pace in nearly one and a half minutes – about the normal time for a seven-furlong event.

The two jockeys kept up their go-slow tactics until they reached the three-furlong post when they started to ride their mounts out. It was Richards who eventually won the day, taking Ridge Wood on to win by three lengths.

The time for the race was a sleep-inducing five minutes fourteen seconds, and although the stewards spoke to the two jockeys, they accepted their explanations for the way they had ridden: they were just following trainers' instructions!

Michael Clayton is Editor of *Horse and Hound*. He is a former reporter for BBC Television News and covered a variety of events world-wide including the war in Vietnam.

PLEASING THE LADIES

At one time I was trying to please two ladies in my life. One of them was a large brown hunter mare, named Betty.

She was an impetuous but enthusiastic performer in the hunting field. Her shortcomings - a disinclination to stand still, and a tendency to buck - were overcome by her ability to gallop endlessly and to jump big obstacles with enthusiasm if not precision.

In order to please the other lady in my life, I promised that she could ride Betty in a hunter trial at the end of the season. We schooled the exuberant mare over the sort of obstacles she was likely to meet.

The lady rider was suitably impressed. Yes, she thought, Betty would give her a good round; might even earn a rosette.

Came the great day. Betty and the keen lady rider went to the start at the hunter trial. An elderly gentleman suddenly signalled that it was Betty's turn to start by waving a huge green flag, almost in her face.

It was too much. Betty bucked, wheeled round - and galloped round the course. Not only did she complete the course the wrong way round, she did it alone. The buck had unseated the other lady I had tried to please.

When I caught Betty she was puffing triumphantly. Clearly she was delighted with her round.

Well, you can't please all the people all the time. The other lady did not stay in my life as long as Betty.

A courageous show jumper but prone to spills

Sebastian Coe is probably the foremost middle distance runner in recent times. He progressed from winning the English Schools' 3,000 metres event at the age of sixteen to breaking world records in the 800 metres, 1,000 metres and the mile. He also won gold and silver medals at both the Moscow and Los Angeles Olympic Games. Seb has a degree in economics, has been a lecturer in physical education and sports science at Loughborough University, and was elected to the Sports Council in 1983.

IM-PATIENT ENCOUNTER

Early in 1978, I suffered a serious injury when I fell down a hole during training at Loughborough. I sat watching my sock expanding like a balloon, and then crawled to a car and was rushed to hospital by my coach, George Gandy.

I was carried pick-a-back 200 yards from the car park to casualty, where it was the usual Sunday scene: kids who'd fallen off swings at the playground, etc.... I sat with my leg in a sling for an hour and eventually was taken to the X-ray department, where the Sister said it was broken. George insisted it wasn't.

Sister: 'I'm telling you it is.'

George: 'I'm not a betting man' (which was a bare-faced lie because he would bet on two earwigs climbing a wall), 'but I'll put my shirt on it that it's not.'

Sister: 'What are your qualifications?'

George: 'MSc in biomechanics.' Whereupon she immediately started calling him 'Dad'.

The X-ray attendant then cheerfully volunteered: 'It's so bad that if it's not broken, it would be better if it was!' The Sister now insisted it should be put in plaster.

George: 'No, there'll be muscle wastage and we won't be able to give him physiotherapy.'

Sister: 'Get out of here at once.' I was then wheeled towards the plaster room.

George: 'Do you realize you are dealing with the fastest 800 metre runner in the world?'

Defiant Sister: 'Well, he'll just have to be the slowest for a change.'

George promptly discharged me, and I subsequently went to see George Preston, a marvellous physiotherapist who used to be with Leicester City FC, and within ten days I was jogging again, which tells you a lot about the quality of sports medicine in general practice in Britain.

SIT IN

During a bantamweight boxing match between South Korean, Jong-il-Byun, and Bulgarian, Aleksandr Hristov, at the Seoul Olympic Games in 1988, the Korean was

54

given two public warnings by the New Zealand referee for illegal use of his head. These obviously made the difference between winning and losing, and the Bulgarian won a majority decision.

This prompted the Korean boxing coach to leap into the ring and begin shouting at the referee. He was followed by a Korean security official who threw a punch. Other officials came to help the referee, and a tug-of-war developed as he was pulled around the ring.

More Koreans joined in, and chairs and equipment were thrown. Finally, the ring was cleared except for Jong-il-Byun who refused to budge. He continued to sit on a stool for more than an hour, even when someone turned the lights off. The Koreans on duty in the stadium then staged a sympathy strike in support of their colleague.

At last, Jong decided that honour had been satisfied and, rising from his stool, he proceeded to bow to all parts of the stadium before leaving the ring.

As a result of the protest, a number of Korean officials were suspended, while the referee – a keen judge of the difference between bravery and stupidity – took the first plane home.

Henry Cooper is probably Britain's most famous heavyweight boxing champion, winning the British, European and Commonwealth titles. In a professional career spanning more than sixteen years he held the British title for a record ten years five months, and became the first man to win the Lonsdale belt three times. In a world title fight, Henry became the first fighter to knock down the then world champion, Muhammad Ali. In 1969, Henry was awarded the OBE for his services to boxing.

THE PLANE TRUTH

I was travelling up to Glasgow to play golf with the late Graham Hill who was flying me up in his plane. I remember that it was plastered with adverts for a tobacco company and the plane was nicknamed 'The flying cigarette packet'.

Graham said to me: 'How high would you like to fly the plane?'

I replied: 'Three foot six inches, because that's my inside leg measurement, and if necessary I can jump out.'

Colin Deans played Rugby for Scotland for ten seasons in the late 70s and 80s, and became the most-capped hooker in the history of the game. His father, Peter Deans, had also played in the same position with considerable success. The young Colin went on to play more than 50 matches for his country, and eight for the British Lions. He captained Scotland 13 times, and also led the Lions in a match against the Rest of the World in 1986. He retired in 1987. In this story he recalls one of the spin-offs of Scotland's 1984 'grand slam' triumphs.

BY APPOINTMENT

There was an unexpected thrill that summer when the 'grand slam' party was invited with their wives to the Queen's Garden Party at Holyrood. We all met for lunch first. To my horror, I found all the rest of the lads were in grey morning suits while I was in black. My wife Val was not at all amused. Imagine my satisfaction, then, to find that once we got to the Palace everyone else was in black and the rest of the boys stood out like sore thumbs.

While we were there Jim Telfer came over to tell us the Duke of Buccleuch wanted to see us. He in turn said the Queen wished to meet the squad and we were escorted to the passageway on the lawn where Her Majesty stopped to speak to various individuals.

During the course of our conversation she remarked that it must be great fun to do nothing but play rugby. I pointed out we all had full-time jobs, and she asked me what I did. I told her I was in the double-glazing business and asked if she was in the market for windows for Holy-rood-house. My joke brought a smile but no order. But I can say that I'm the only double-glazing man to have tried to sell windows to the Queen!

Colin also recalls the preparations for his first match as captain of Scotland, against France in 1986:
On the night before the match, we went to the cinema to relax. The manager was kind enough to announce at the interval that the Scottish team was present and to ask the audience to wish us well. It was a nice gesture, and everyone applauded.

It was only spoiled by one punter in front of me who turned round and said eagerly: 'Which yin of youse is Kenny Dalglish?' Well, there's no accounting for taste.

HAPPINESS IS A CIGAR ...

In 1933 an American swimmer, Charles Zibelman, announced that he planned to swim the English Channel. Nothing unusual about that, except that Zibelman had no legs. As if this wasn't enough of a handicap, he declared that he would also smoke fifty cigars on the way. Zibelman was making good progress until, after twelve hours, he was forced to retire after being badly stung on the mouth by a jellyfish.

Marathon events also appealed to a Lebanese surf-board rider called Bahige Zuhairy who once decided to paddle his board across the Mediterranean. He set out from Beirut in September 1964 with an escort ship and began paddling his way towards Cyprus. After one day at sea, the maritime Little and Large ran into rough weather. The escort vessel, a forty foot cruiser, lost both engines in the heavy seas, and began to drift. As a result, the crew lost sight of Zuhairy and feared the worst. The vessel was eventually rescued and towed into port by a tugboat.

Meanwhile Zuhairy, with rather more stamina than his escort, had continued to paddle, and without the aid of supporting vessel – or compass – reached Cyprus less than two days after setting out from Beirut.

Eddie 'The Eagle' Edwards is a ski jumper who holds the British 90 metre record with a jump of 71 metres. He came from nowhere to represent Great Britain in the Winter Olympics in Calgary in 1988 where he leapt to last place. But in personifying the Olympic ideal of having taken part, he developed a cult following around the world. Even President Reagan became a fan, and delayed an important meeting so he could see Eddie jump. He now has his eye on winning a medal at the 1992 Winter Olympics.

THE EAGLE'S HELMET HAS LANDED

Before the 1988 Olympics, I was training very hard in Kanersteg, Switzerland, and had at last progressed to the 90 metre jump. My helmet was, unfortunately, quite old and the only way I could keep it on was with some string!

I had prepared myself to make my longest jump so far, and after a period of deep concentration at the start, I launched myself off the jump as hard as I could. Unfortunately, at that moment, the string

on the helmet snapped, and it flew off my head.
   I really should have hung on to it ... I managed
to jump 54 metres, *but the helmet managed 93!*

ⓜ

Matthew Engel is an award-winning sports columnist on the *Guardian*. He has a deserved reputation as an acute and witty cricket correspondent, but has reported on more than sixty different sports around the world in addition to such unsporting events as general elections. He is co-author of an annual sports almanac, and author of a number of other books. Here is the account he wrote of one of English cricket's great fiascos, on the New Zealand tour of 1983-84.

ENGLAND DESERVE THE BIRD

February 1984

Christchurch: shortly before the end came in the second Test yesterday, the seagulls that had been perched on top of the Christchurch scoreboard all through the match suddenly flew down, en masse and squawking, almost on to the square itself. They have a finely tuned instinct for rubbish.

The argument that will persist about this game will concern which was the more trashy: the pitch or England's performance on it. Before considering that, one has to take in the magnitude of

England's defeat, a humiliation so complete that it boggles the mind. England lost by an innings and 132 runs, which is not unprecedented in Tests against Australia or the modern West Indies. But this was against New Zealand.

England were bowled out for 82 and 93. There are only five previous instances since the First World War of England's being bowled out even once in a Test match for under 100. It has not happened twice in a match this century.

And it all happened so quickly. England's last three-day Test was twelve years ago (victory over Australia at Leeds in 1972). But there was no play before 4.30 this Saturday. The match finished yesterday at 4.31 precisely. Except for the one minute, it was a two-day Test. England had lost in two days in 1921 to Warwick Armstrong's brilliant Australians. This – you almost have to pinch yourself as you repeat it – was against New Zealand, who until six years ago had never beaten England at all.

There is no doubt that it was a bad wicket, but both teams had to play on the same pitch. It may perhaps have been a shade moist on Saturday afternoon after the rain. Willis thought it was deteriorating fast. Geoff Howarth, the New Zealand captain, thought it was actually playing a little more reliably yesterday.

The two captains had analysed the situation very differently before the match. Willis concluded that it would be a waste of time playing a spin bowler and on Friday condoned – or did nothing to stop – a policy of constant short pitching. The

New Zealanders decided that Steve Boock, the slow left-armer, could play an important part – and he did, especially in undermining the confidence of England's two left-handers, Fowler and Gower, as the bowler's footmarks turned into rough outside their off-stump.

New Zealand also reasoned that if they bowled a full length in the region of off-stump to all the batsmen on this pitch, they could let the ball do the work and wait for the nicks. Thirteen of the twenty England wickets fell to catches between wicket-keeper and gully, all expertly taken.

But it remains quite staggering that an England team, including an extra batsman against just this sort of contingency, could muster only fourteen boundaries (several of those off the edge) and 175 runs in two innings lasting for just six hours. This is not a bad England batting team. Names like Gower and Botham will ring down the ages for their deeds on other occasions.

But the game of cricket is played inside the players' heads as much as it is played on a twenty-two-yard strip, and it is in their heads that England lost this game. They had decided the situation was hopeless and so, inevitably, hopeless it became.

There was not much that could be done to retrieve England's first innings yesterday. They resumed at fifty-three for seven, needing to get 108 to avoid the follow-on, and never looked like doing it. Gatting, who had gone in at No 7 because of a damaged shoulder, avoided getting out. The tail put up as much resistance as could reasonably be expected and England were all out 225 runs behind at 12.15.

Howarth did not think long before making England bat again. Fowler and Tavaré walked out to face 35 minutes before lunch and at first nothing went wrong. It was a cool cloudy day. Would England battle it out and hope that rain might return? Not a chance. Many of these batsmen have an adequate technique but dubious attitude. With Tavaré, the reverse may be true. He stepped back, dangled the bat at Hadlee and was caught behind.

Gower, who more than anyone gave the impression that the pitch might leap up and bite him, pushed forward and was caught at fourth slip; Fowler was again out to Boock, to a ball that bounced more than he expected, which he pushed to silly point; Gatting cover-drove and thick-edged to first slip.

Enter Botham, this time without his first-innings helmet. Boock flighted the first ball, Botham on-drove, got an inside edge and found Martin Crowe's left hand at forward short leg. Thirty-one for five.

Randall, on a pair, avoided the hat-trick. Then Coney scooped up a catch at second slip to remove Lamb. Thirty-three for six. Then after 16 wickets came a little resistance from Randall and Taylor, two instinctive fighters. The stand was broken unluckily, Taylor slipping as he changed his mind about a single into the covers. Seventy-two for seven.

By now Hadlee was back in the attack and there was no batting to come. Even Randall could not fight on, and was caught by one of the predatory gullies. Cowans had a brief slog, edged, and it was all over. There was time for Piggott, if he could uncancel the invitations, to go ahead and have his wedding today as planned. But who among this lot would you choose as best man?

LEARNING THE HARD WAY

Viv Richards once reputedly played and missed against an aspiring fast bowler who promptly made the mistake of giving the master a description of what he had been aiming at. 'It's red and it's round,' he said.

Richards immediately walked down the wicket and clattered the bowler's next delivery out of the ground and down the road, remarking to his taunter: 'Since you know what it looks like, you go and get it.'

'Oh, NO! Not another Sumo wrestler!'

A famous rugby club was said to have been approached by a major firm of dog food manufacturers with a view to entering into a sponsorship agreement. Alas, the deal broke down when the club – going through a particularly bad patch – discovered they would be required to display the manufacturer's brand name on the front of their jerseys – WINALOT.

A Scottish Post Office rugby team went off on tour armed with line-out codes worked out on the basis that the name of an Irish town would be the signal for the ball to be thrown to the front; a Welsh town indicated the back. And what did the geographically retarded P O hooker call at the first line-out of the match? Why, 'Bangor' of course.

The 1990-91 season was a traumatic one for Hibernian FC who survived a takeover bid but became the only senior club in Britain not to achieve an away league win. Their fortunes were summed up by one supporter, who remarked: 'Hibs have sixty-six players on their books – that's a team for every day of the week except Saturday.'

John Frame (Highland, Edinburgh University and Gala) played rugby for Scotland on twenty-three occasions as a centre/three-quarter in the late 1960s and early seventies. Today he is a stockbroker in Edinburgh, and runs The Sportman's Charity, which has raised more than £130,000 for disabled and handicapped sports people and for children's charities.

A POLISHED PERFORMANCE

Attitudes towards amateurism have changed a great deal since I played rugby – and probably not before time. In those days, even at international level, Scots players provided their own shorts and stockings. Then, if at the end of a match, you swapped your jersey you had to foot the bill for a new one – an exorbitant eight guineas. Equally, any expenses for a match were scrutinized carefully by the secretary of the Scottish Rugby Union before settlement.

On one occasion, one of my former team mates, Peter Stagg, the 6 ft 10 ins Sale second-row forward, fell foul of the Secretary when he put in an expenses sheet which included 10 shillings and 6 pence for a copy of *Playboy* which he had bought to read while travelling to Edinburgh.When he received his cheque, he saw that the Secretary had put his red pencil through the claim for the magazine. Peter was very annoyed, and before the next day's international, he determined to sort out what he thought was the unnecessary meanness of the SRU.

As we sat in the dressing room just before the match, the President of the SRU, Wilson Shaw, the former Scottish fly half, came in to give us a brief pep-talk. Everyone was ready for the match, except Peter who was sitting there without his boots, and with his stockings still around his ankles.

As Wilson began to speak, 'Staggy' pulled out his kitbag and produced a tin of boot polish which he noisily dropped on the concrete floor. He then pulled up one sock to reveal a hole extending from ankle to knee. As Wilson continued his talk, all eyes were on Peter who ostentatiously began to apply polish to the part of his leg not covered by the dark-blue stocking.

Peter's message was quite clear, and by the time he had finished, everyone, including the President, was rocking with restrained mirth. As he left, Wilson turned to the Secretary with instructions to fetch Peter a new pair of stockings.

Ⓜ

David Frith is editor of *Wisden Cricket Monthly* and author of numerous cricket books, his most recent on cricketers who have committed suicide!

KEEPING UP WITH THE GAME

Wicketkeepers, they say, are a crazy lot. They take most of the knocks during a cricket match: fingers broken by rearing balls, ribs bruised, big toes chipped, eyebrows lacerated by over-eager batsmen who have no control over the follow-through to their hook shot. But wicketkeepers are usually good to have around, for they're traditionally chirpy and conversational and encouraging. Imagine, then, having *three* of them on the field at the same time! And in a *first-class-match!*

It was at Leyton in 1971, and I think it remains unique in cricket history. Essex were batting, Somerset fielding, when their wicketkeeper, Derek Taylor, was hit in the mouth. His captain, the mighty, bald and bold Brian Close, was by his side assisting him in seconds. But there was too much blood coming from Taylor's mouth, and he had to run from the field for medical attention.

The skipper looked round and decided that Roy

Virgin was the best bet as a substitute wicketkeeper, so Virgin trotted off to get the pads on, Brian Close meanwhile eagerly pulling on the wicket-keeping gloves (fearlessly shunning pads), taking over until Virgin returned.

Close was having the time of his life behind the stumps. It's demanding enough fielding at 'suicide point', but, somehow, keeping wicket with no leg-guards or protective 'box' demanded even greater bravery – some would insist stupidity.

Suddenly, Virgin appeared at the gate, tugging on the gloves, fully padded up, ready to run back onto the field at the end of the over. Close was so absorbed in his new duties that he failed to notice him, even when he had reached the pitch. When the Somerset players pointed out that the substitute wicketkeeper had arrived, their captain seemed extremely reluctant to forsake the gloves.

And at that point who should come back onto the field but the original keeper, Taylor, mouth stuffed with cotton-wool to stem the flow of blood. This seemed momentarily to persuade Brian Close that since Virgin and Taylor couldn't make up their minds, he might as well carry on keeping wicket: it really was proving to be a fulfilling way of passing the afternoon, he seemed to think.

If only there had been a camera to hand. For those precious few moments we had three wicketkeepers staring at each other, the game frozen in its progress. With glowering reluctance Close eventually pulled off the gloves; Virgin skipped back to the pavilion to disrobe; and Taylor, indestructible, resumed his perilous post.

BUSH JUSTICE

No jockey in horse-racing can ever have experienced a faster application of justice than a rider called Jimmy Dunne who rode in an event on a country track in Queensland, Australia, in 1915.

At a meeting held by the Springsure Jockey Club, the chief steward, Frank McGill, had a hunch that Dunne did not plan to try his best on his mount, Soldier Lad. He spoke to the jockey, but was still not convinced that the horse would be given every chance.

As the riders were lining up for the five furlong event, Mr McGill borrowed a horse which had already raced in an earlier event, and rode over to the start.

Soon after the riders were sent on their way, Dunne was seen to fall off Soldier Lad. However, before he had even had time to climb to his feet, the chief steward galloped up, and informed him he had been suspended from riding for twelve months.

Nick Gillingham has continued the Great British tradition of producing champion breastroke swimmers. In 1989 he broke world, European and Commonwealth records for the stroke. Today he is still the European open champion and current British, Commonwealth and European record holder in the 200 metres event.

'TAKE YOUR BLOCKS ...'

In 1979, when I was a pure novice of just twelve, I was taking part in the local open meet along with many top Midland age-groupers.Shaking from head to toe with nerves, I stood on the back of my starting block as the whistle sounded for quiet. The starter had a deafening regimental voice, which didn't help, and as I took my mark I grabbed on to my starting block.

As that moment I discovered it had not been fixed to the poolside. Not only did I false start, but my block also ended up under fourteen feet of water. It was cast iron, and I had to collect it from the bottom of the swimming pool before the race could continue.

Needless to say, I was greatly embarrassed, and ended up losing the race.

Moments before tragedy struck at the pool

CAP THIS

Some shattering defeats on tour in Australia in the lead up to the 1991 rugby World Cup saw Welsh coach Ron Waldron accused of making panic changes. One bemused Taffy claimed: 'The Kuwaitis will be wanting Ron Waldron to quell their oil wells – he'll cap anything.'

Graham Gooch is the current England and
Essex cricket captain. A high-scoring right-
hand batsman and useful medium pace
bowler, he has played more than eighty
Tests since 1975. His highest score was 333
against India in 1990, a match in which he
set a record of 456 for the aggregate number
of runs in both innings. He has made ten
overseas tours for England.

PLANNING AHEAD

Keith Fletcher – 'Fletch' – who was my captain at Essex for a number of years, was
also captain of the England touring side
when we went to India in 1981-82.

He was not keen on team meetings, and I cannot
recall a single occasion when he called us together
to discuss an individual Essex match. When he led
England, however, some meetings were clearly
essential and I well remember the occasion when
he called the bowlers together before the Second
Test in Bangalore during the Indian tour.

We were already one down and Keith wanted to
sort out fields and tactics against each of the
Indian batsmen as we tried to manoeuvre the
equalizing win. The trouble was, every time a

batsman's name was mentioned, Ian Botham would take over:

'Don't worry about him, I'll bounce him out.'

'He can't play the short ball.'

'He's scared of my bouncer, I'll take care of him!'

And so we went through the team, the rest of us convulsed with laughter as Ian won the Test single-handed with the short-pitched bowling of which is is so fond. History relates that India only batted once in the Bangalore Test, scoring 428 with Ian taking 2 for 137...but his confidence is not something we ever discouraged.

PLAYING FOR BOTH SIDES

It's not unusual for footballers to play against their old clubs after transferring to another team, but it must be rare for a player to represent both sides in the same match.

In December 1932, J Oakes turned out for the second division club, Port Vale against Charlton Athletic. However, the game had to be abandoned because of the deepening winter gloom before it was completed. By the time the fixture could be rearranged, Oakes had transferred to Charlton, and he found himself playing in the same match against his old side.

Duncan Goodhew vowed from an early age that he would become an Olympic champion. At school he had been taunted by the other children because a fall from a tree at the age of ten had left him bald, and because he was dyslexic. His determined will to win helped him to succeed David Wilkie as Britain's leading breaststroke swimmer, and also brought him gold at the 1980 Olympic Games.

FLYING THE FLAG

I was very keen to represent my country at the 1980 Olympic Games in Moscow because I was certain I could improve on my performance in the 1976 Games, and perhaps take the gold medal for the 100 metres breaststroke. I had been studying in America, but decided to return to Britain ten months before the Games so that nobody could claim that my victory – should I be lucky enough to achieve it – was simply because of superior American training methods.

There was a lot of soul searching among many of the British athletes before they decided to take part in the Games. A number of countries, including the United States, had withdrawn because of the Soviet invasion of Afghanistan. The British government urged the country's athletes not to take part, but many of us believed that it was unfair to place such moral pressure on us. There was a very serious debate on the issue in my family, and my stepfather decided he would not go to Moscow in support of the Government's stand.

Happily, however, my mother did decide to come and watch, and she was well and truly there when I took my place in the final. All the way through the race, the British supporters were chanting, 'Goodhew . . . Goodhew . . .' But in spite of all the noise, I am sure I could hear my mother's voice above the din urging me on.

After trailing for the first part of the race, I came through to win by just under half a second from a Russian and an Australian. I would have loved my father, who had died eight years earlier, to have been there, but in his memory I wore his old flat cap for the medal presentation.

I was very proud to have won the Gold for Britain, but was rather disappointed that, in view of the political opinion at home, the Olympic flag rather than the Union Jack was raised to mark my victory for Britain. However, in an ironical twist, the Union Jack was displayed anyway – flying beside ours, as part of the Australian flag raised for Peter Evans, the swimmer who had come in third.

Ⓜ

David Gower is one of the most gifted batsmen to have played for England for many years. He has played more than a hundred Test matches, thirty-two of them as captain, and has made fifteen overseas tours. He has scored nearly fifty first class centuries, and has passed 1,000 runs in a season on eleven occasions. Sometimes accused of appearing too casual about the game, David nevertheless has an affection for its characters and history – as his choice of this story shows:

THERE BUT FOR THE GRACE...

There can be few players in the recent history of cricket who can have dominated the game as Dr W.G. Grace did last century. He always made a substantial impact wherever he went, but on his first visit to Australia with an England team in 1874 the life of one of his Australian opponents was dramatically changed – and certainly not for the best. Unlike today's carefully planned visits, that tour had a certain amount of flexibility. Because of this, the England team was persuaded to travel from Melbourne to South Australia to play an unscheduled match.

The people of Adelaide had been demanding such an event because they were desperately keen to see the legendary Dr Grace. Reluctantly, he agreed to play in a three-day game for the small consideration of £110 and half the gate.

The game created tremendous excitement in Adelaide, starved of top-class cricket as the town was, and the Englishmen lined up against a South Australian XI. The local side made 63 and 82, and the English XI 108 and 38 for 3, to win by seven wickets. However the sensation of the game was the dismissal of the great Dr Grace, caught one-handed on the boundary by a local bank clerk, Alex Crooks, for just six runs. Grace insisted the ball had been caught beyond the boundary, and that he was not out. However, the umpire could not be budged and the Englishman returned to the pavilion protesting bitterly.

Because of his triumph, Crooks' fame spread. The directors of his bank were so impressed that when they needed a new general manager their cricket hero was duly appointed. Unfortunately his skill on the field did not translate to his management of the bank, and within four years it had lost more than £1,160,000. Investigations revealed that the cricket-manager had been less than scrupulous in handling its funds. He was sentenced to eight years in prison, and the ailing bank went into liquidation.

I suppose it could be said that few catches in the long history of cricket can have had such disastrous results.

Colin Hart has been boxing and athletics correspondent for the *Sun* newspaper since it started more than twenty years ago, and was boxing correspondent for its predecessor. During the past twenty-five years he has covered dozens of world championship fights around the world, following the careers of such champions as Muhammad Ali, Sugar Ray Leonard, Roberto Duran, Frank Bruno and Barry McGuigan. He has also covered every Olympic Games since Mexico City in 1968.

SAFETY FIRST

One of my favourite stories from boxing seems to sum up the often crazy world of the fight game. It was told to me by Dick Sadler, a black Californian with a gravel voice like Louis Armstrong, who used to be a vaudeville artist.

Sadler managed many fighters but he will always be famous for taking George Foreman to the heavyweight championship of the world.

Back in the 1960s in Omaha, Nebraska, Mel Turnbow, a young giant heavyweight was being built up as a 'white hope'. He had a string of quick knock-out wins to his credit – but they were achieved mostly against stiffs and set-ups.

Sadler was at his Los Angeles home when one day he got a call from Turnbow's people. Dick said: 'They asked me if I could provide someone capable of going at least five rounds with Turnbow.

'I said I could, and after some haggling over money and expenses the deal was done. Then I telephoned one of my older fighters – a guy who wasn't very good, and I told him I had a job for him.

'I explained the deal and that he had to go to Omaha, and last five rounds with Turnbow. He sounded horrified – he said: "You know very well, Dick, I've never gone more than three rounds with anyone in my life."

'But I managed to convince him he had nothing to worry about and when I told him how much he was going to earn, he agreed the fight.

'When we arrived in Omaha, it didn't take long to realize the only black things in the town were the hearses. And when we got to the arena on the night, the place was packed to the rafters with thousands of hostile rednecks.

'They were anticipating another spectacular victory for the local hero.'

Dick Sadler went on: 'Soon after the bell sounded for the first round it was obvious Turnbow was a bit of a palooka. That message got through to my guy as well, and suddenly he hit Turnbow on the chin with a big right, and over he went.

'As he lay on the canvas, there was a deathly hush, and I prayed that Mel not only got back on

his feet but that he lasted until the end of the
round.

'Fortunately he did both, and when my guy got
back to the corner, I yelled at him: "What the hell
are you trying to do – get us both lynched?" I told
him I was retiring him. He shouted: "Sheeet, Dick,
I can knock him out."

'That's exactly what I was afraid of, and decided
I wasn't going to take any more chances.

'Desperately I tried to attract the attention of the
referee who was marking his scorecard in one of
the neutral corners – oblivious to my yelling.

'So I threw the towel in the ring, then I threw
the sponge in the ring, and in my desperation, I
threw the bucket in the ring.

'The referee, realizing something was up,
marched across and said: "You got a problem?"

'I told him I was retiring my man. He said:
"What for? There doesn't seem to be anything
wrong with him."

'I said: "Oh yes there is – he's bleeding." "I can't
see any blood," said the ref. "That's because he's
bleeding internally," I replied.

'We lost. But at least we got out of town with
our lives still intact,' Dick Sadler said.

*Colin Hart also shares some of his memories of the
former world middleweight champion, Terry Downes:*
Terry Downes was one of the fight game's greatest
characters and his Cockney humour had many a
dressing room rocking with laughter. The former
champion was a popular fighter with the fans

from the beginning of his career which started in 1957.

Old timers reckoned he reminded them of the crashing, dashing style of the legendary Ted 'Kid' Lewis.

Downes, in his third pro fight, was featured in a main event against Dick Tiger, a Liverpool-based Nigerian at Shoreditch Town Hall, in London's East End.

Terry was an overwhelming favourite as Tiger had lost four of his first five fights. But it turned out to be a tremendous battle with both men on the floor.

In the end, Tiger proved too good for Downes who was retired with a cut eye in the fifth round. As it was such an upset, Downes' dressing room was packed with boxing writers.

Tiger had been slightly overweight at the weigh-in, and Terry's connections were making a great play of this. One of the pressmen asked Downes if he thought Tiger looked a big middleweight.

'Yeah', said Downes. 'He looked a big middleweight to me too – but then I realized I was lying down, and he was standing up.'

When he was asked who he would like to fight next, Tel – quick as a flash – said: 'The bleedin' match-maker.'

I remember too the morning after Downes stopped Paul Pender to win the world crown at Wembley. He was holding court for the press at his Paddington car showroom.

Among the throng of sportswriters was a young

girl reporter from the *Evening News*. She felt out of it as she knew nothing about boxing, but she was determined to ask a question.

Bursting to the front she confronted Terry who was sitting on the bonnet of a car. 'Mr Downes,' she said, 'I understand some boxers look at their opponents' eyes when they are in the ring while others look at their gloves. What do you look at?'

'Well, darling,' said Tel, 'to tell you the truth, I always look at their gloves.'

'Why's that?' she asked. 'Because,' said Downes, 'I ain't been hit by an eye yet.'

During the Liverpool manager's rather tempestuous footballing career his name became synonymous with a form of refreshment in the Glasgow pubs.

Anyone asking for a 'Graeme Souness' intended to have a 'quick half and then off'.

THE DAY HIS NUMBER CAME UP

For some years now, computer rankings have been very important in determining who qualifies for Wimbledon. Being 128 or 129 on the computer can mean the difference between playing in the All England Championships or missing out. If someone drops out, the next person on the computer will be entitled to take their place.

One of the most popular players to appear at Wimbledon in the 1970s and 80s was Vijay Amritraj who was also making his name at the time as a film star. In 1983, he played a role in the James Bond film, *Octopussy*, with Roger Moore. By coincidence, the gala première was held in London just before Wimbledon, and Vijay decided to take a party of tennis players along to the event at a cinema in Leicester Square. One member of the party was Bruce Kleege, a tall American who, because of his computer ranking, was first reserve to play at Wimbledon in the event of any vacancies.

As they sat watching the film, the players saw their friend Vijay, who was playing James Bond's colleague, get killed on the screen. At that moment, Bruce Kleege leaped to his feet shouting: 'I'm in! I'm in!'

Michael Herd is assistant editor and head of sport at the London *Evening Standard*. He has been the *Standard*'s sports editor, news editor and assistant editor (news), and during a five-year spell away from Fleet Street, was editor-in-chief of a provincial group with twenty-three titles.

THE EXPLODING HORSE

'The trouble wi' zis 'orse,' said Jaroslav Wesely, 'is zat sometime somet'ing changes in 'is 'ead. Zat is when he becomes a really cheeky fellow.

'He has too much life, zis one. Sometimes 'e is like a dynamite. Bang! Like exploding. Yes, he is really strong but sometime, unfortunately, he is confused up 'ere,' Wesely explained, tapping his head with his right forefinger.

At the time we were sitting on bales of straw in a horse-box at the Paddock Stables, Aintree. Mr Wesely was sipping champagne from a glass compliments of the Aintree management and I was swigging fiery, stomach-stoking slivovitz from a bottle compliments of the Co-operative Farm of Slusovice in Czechoslavakia.

Mr Wesely and three other members of the Co-operative had arrived at Aintree an hour earlier after three days on the road driving from Moravia in central Czechoslavakia, through Germany and Belgium to Liverpool with the most unusual entry for the 1986 Grand National

Despite its English name, Essex, the horse was an eight-year-old stallion bred in Russia and bought in Hungary by the Co-operative. It was the first Czech horse to run in the National since the Thirties.

Brake trouble outside Munich, several flat tyres and a spot of bother with a customs officer at Dover had not prevented the Czechs from arriving at Aintree right on time.

'Ve are four here. I am the veterinary surgeon and translator and here is Mr Vaclav Chaloupka, who is one of the foremost riders in our country, jah. Ve have a groom and the old man standing over there is the watch-man. He vill sleep wi' the horse. He must. It is his duty.'

Essex was a large raw-boned stallion with a large moon-shaped scar on his hind quarter. Everything was stacked against him. He hadn't run for months and he had never seen a barricade called Becher's or any of the other thirty fences that comprise the National.

The bookies were offering 200-1 against Essex winning and tens against him even finishing. The Czechs just shrugged. Steeplechase jockeys are the same the world over.

'Mr Chaloupka ask me to tell you he is not nervous and he ask me to tell you he is not worry. He drop down a lot of times off horses but he always wake up. Mr Chaloupka vill vin.'

Mr Wesely, Mr Chaloupka and the Slusovice slivovitz were very convincing so I put a tenner on the nose at 200-1 and a tenner that the Czechs would finish; a mouth-watering promise of £2,000.

Come the race, Essex soared like a stag. He did not fall at Becher's and Mr Chaloupka did not drop down off the horse. I would like to tell you they won but they didn't.

The Czech horse was pulled up at the 15th, beaten not by the course and not by his rivals but by a broken girth buckle. I lost my money and Essex disappeared back to central Moravia.

FORTY-NINE REASONS TO CELEBRATE

Football teams which throw everything into attack are likely to score, but run the risk of letting the opposition score as well. Two village teams playing in a match in Frankfurt, Germany, had every reason to go for goals in a match in 1949 – they had been promised a bottle of schnapps for every goal scored. As a result both teams put on a superb display of attacking football. The result was 25-24!

> Ⓜ
>
> **Rachael Heyhoe Flint** was captain of the
> England Women's Cricket team until 1979,
> having first played for her country in 1960.
> She also played international hockey,
> coached in the USA, and has written several
> hockey coaching books. She is a freelance
> journalist and broadcaster, and in 1972 was
> awarded the MBE for services to cricket –
> the first woman to gain such an honour.

DURDEN DOUBLE DUTCH

The *faux pas* produced with hilarious rapidity
by Brian Johnston while lightening and
brightening up our cricket listening on Test
Match Special, are legion. But I believe I was involved in one of the most embarrassingly funny
comments in decades of sport broadcasting.

Picture the scene: Wembley Stadium in March
1974 for the annual Women's Hockey International
with 65,000 screaming schoolgirl spectators and
many accompanying teachers with headaches.
England were playing The Netherlands, and I was
working with the commentary team on ITV's live
presentation of the women's hockey showpiece on
its *World of Sport* programme.

The main commentator was Neil Durden-Smith.
My job was to sit there like W. Barrington Dalby

(late of boxing commentary fame) coming in with the inter-round summaries and pithy tactical explanations. (I have to confess that, being a former England goalkeeper as opposed to a field player, my tactical knowledge was somewhat vague.)

With about ten minutes remaining, England were attacking desperately, trying to erase Holland's 2-0 lead, but time was obviously against them. Neil was getting really stuck into his commentary, and becoming more and more excited. Helma Hoegen, the Netherlands goalkeeper, was in the thick of the action, repelling England's valiant efforts with a string of magnificent saves.

At this point, Neil was waxing lyrical about Helma's skill and expertise, and the whole world of viewing millions must have been absolutely lifted off their chairs at home when Neil remarked:

'What a magnificent player Hoegen is...marvellous saves...she's a medical assistant, a very experienced international – and she's got thirty-one Dutch caps!!'

Which probably accounted for the funny way she ran.

⊛

Tony Higgins has been Secretary of the Scottish Professional Footballers' Association for more than five years following a distinguished playing career with four Scottish clubs – Hibs, Partick Thistle, Morton and Stranraer (where he was player/coach) – over nearly twenty years.

EXPENSIVE MISTAKE

During my time at Partick Thistle from 1980 to 1982, I was managed by Bertie Auld, the former Celtic and Scotland player. He was also a member of the first British team to win the European Cup.

Bertie was one of the great characters of Scottish football and he had a quick humour which was to become legendary among football players in Scotland. I recall a Scottish Cup tie when Partick, a Premier League side, was playing a lowly second division team.

One of our players had a particularly bad game that day, and was constantly barracked by the supporters. In the dressing room after the game, Bertie immediately picked on the player.

'Hey son, the punters are all shouting that you're useless, daft and stupid. But don't worry son, you're not usless, daft or stupid. I am. I paid forty grand for you.'

> **Jimmy Hill** is one of football's best-known faces, appearing regularly on BBC Television as an expert summarizer. His knowledge of the game comes from a long career as a player with Fulham and Brentford, and as Manager and then Chairman of Coventry City, Chairman of Charlton, and currently as Chairman of Fulham. He once scored five goals in an away match against Doncaster.

CANDID CAMERA

This is not so much a sporting story as a television story linked with sport describing a minor catastrophe. The programme concerned was called *Sportswide* and it used to go out at 6.45 on Friday evenings as part of that very fine programme, *Nationwide*. The programme itself was performed live, but the section containing the previous Saturday's football action was recorded in the afternoon and put together in an eight-minute package. As presenter of *Sportswide*, I would refer very briefly to the football tape, activated by a command from the show's editor, and the button would be pressed by the technician in the videotape suite. After that segment, we were then due to return live for an interview with Peter

O'Sullevan who would preview the following afternoon's racing, and give the odd tip or two.

On the evening of the catastrophe, I had to change my place from the opening position to one at the other end of the curved desk for the final interview with Peter O'Sullevan. Between us were Michael Barratt, Sue Lawley and Bob Wellings, the *Nationwide* presenters of the evening. In order to make the move I had to unplug and take with me my microphone lead and what is referred to in television as a 'deaf aid'. This provides a direct link between the editor and the presenter so that instructions can be passed on during the pro-gramme.

On that evening I had performed my opening link into the football package – perhaps 'Arsenal and Spurs fought out a most interesting 2-2 draw last Saturday – here are the goals coming up now.' Having read the link and taken a quick look at the monitor to see that the Spurs and Arsenal players were running around on the screen, I pulled my deaf aid and microphone from their sockets ready to move to the position for my interview with Peter O'Sullevan.

I put my pipe in my mouth and proceeded to light it. At that point, Sue Lawley hissed urgently at me: 'You're on the screen Jimmy!' I looked at the screen and to my horror there I was lighting my pipe, the footballers having disappeared. Because I was no longer connected to the editor, I did not know what had gone wrong, or how long the problem would continue before the videotape was rolling again.

The other facet to the story was that I had agreed to drive after that evening's show to the National Equestrian Centre in Stoneleigh, Warwickshire, to take part in a charity show jumping event. As time was limited, I was already dressed in my jodhpurs and riding boots. In the desperation of the moment, I decided to stand up, show the viewers my riding breeches, and tell them about the charity event until the fault was put right.

I stood up boldly and said: 'I've got something to show you down here, and I want to let let you into a little secret.' At that moment Sue said: 'Good heavens, Jimmy, it's not that desperate.' She had seen, but I had not, that the footballers were once more restored to the screen. Although the viewers had caught sight of my pipe, they fortunately did not see the jodhpurs, or hear my proud statement.

What had happened was that the videotape operator, having pressed the button to start the action, had felt momentarily that he had made a mistake and pressed another button to stop the tape. Out of my hearing, it had not taken long for the editor to get the programme on course again.

Ten minutes later, I was on course for the NEC and a clear round – I like to think!

Martin Johnson is the cricket correspondent for the *Independent*, and has travelled extensively to cover the game. He has brought a distinctive style to cricket reporting, and has developed a large following among the readers of the paper. In this piece he looks back on the season of 1990 when bowlers came close to despair in:

THE YEAR OF THE BAT

The sun was not always beating down on parched outfields (for much of the New Zealand series it rained), neither was the scoreboard always registering 900 for no wicket (after England's first ball of the summer it was 0 for 1), but 1990 was indisputably the Year of the Bat.

Lord's had already acted in 1989 to prevent the medium pacer from inheriting the earth, by making the earth subject to 25-point penalties. To this they added a clause outlawing a ball with stitching prouder than a Mohican haircut, and the end product was runs, runs, and more runs. So many runs, in fact, that batsmen barely bothered to doff the helmet unless they passed 200, and in anguished acknowledgement of the fact that it had become easier to get past a Lord's gateman than an outside edge, the Middlesex bowler Simon Hughes suggested extending Law 42 to include intimidatory batting.

The orgy began in May, when a Surrey total of 707 – the best by a county since 1934 – resulted in a first innings deficit of 156. Lancashire's reply of 863 was the third highest first-class total ever made in this country, and so it went on.

As the sun grew hotter, people who claimed they had even seen the Test team scoring mountains of runs were treated for delirium. It was, however, no mirage. After four summers without so much as a single Test win, England, on a tidal wave of runs from their captain, won both series.

Graham Gooch, the first man to score 1,000 runs in an English Test summer, celebrated these collective and individual triumphs in his customary over-the-top manner. Having contributed 456 runs, a couple of catches, a wicket and a run-out in England's win over India at Lord's, Gooch shuffled into the press conference clutching a can of Diet Coke, and upon being invited to compare his team to the 1938 Australians, murmured something to the effect that England had the makings of a goodish side; maybe.

The move to eradicate poor pitches is working, although there is evidence that the TCCB has gone too far the other way with the ball, because not even the spinners can get a proper purchase on it. The 1989 county champions, Worcestershire, collected 83 bonus points for bowling, while this year's winners, Middlesex, picked up only 55.

They are worthy three-day champions, but the

competition as a whole has become increasingly devalued by artificial three-day contests in which insertions were almost always made with declarations and a final afternoon run-chase in mind. The next year's *Wisden* would contain a footnote underneath the entry listing Tom Moody's 26-minute century for Warwickshire, making specific reference to the assortment of deliberate rubbish purveyed at him in the 'interests' of trying to obtain a result.

Batsmen have never had a summer like it. Gooch's 333 will remain in the memory for a long time, as will Azharuddin's 87-minute century in the same Test match, when wrists like revolving doors sent the ball off in almost any direction he pleased. Then there was Kapil Dev, with 24 required to save the follow-on, lashing four consecutive sixes off Hemmings into the Nursery End scaffolding and threatening to put back work on the New Compton and Edrich stands by another year.

There were 15 centuries in 15 days' play between England and India, one of them enabling Sachin Tenduklar to become the second youngest centurion in Test history, and the last of the 15 sparing David Gower, ol' blue socks himself, from what might have been the final curtain.

Even Devon Malcolm batted for nearly an hour in a Test innings, and gone are the days when a tail-ender, pushing studiously forward like a proper batsman, was given out for 'false pretences'. Well, almost gone. Members of the Society for the Preservation of Real No 11s can raise a glass to

Northamptonshire's Mark Robinson, almost as hopeless a batsman as the Cobblers' legendary Jim Griffiths. Robinson broke the world record for duff batting by going 12 first-class innings without scoring.

Finally, if 1990 was the year of the bat, it was also the year of the sponsor. England's shirts are soon to flogged off, and the Oval Test saw the unveiling of two painted logos on prime television spots in the outfield. If Richard Hadlee was grateful for one thing, it was in retiring before his 431st and last Test wicket (Malcolm) could be preserved in the archives for future generations with the message to shop at Tesco.

NOT IN THE RACE

Spectators at sporting events are often critical of decisions by judges, umpires or referees – but seldom have the last word.

However, at a race meeting in Brisbane, Australia, more than sixty years ago, the judge was so astray in his decision that the sport's ruling body had no alternative but to change it.

Mr Arthur Drury was described as 'one of the greatest and most conscientious of judges in horse racing', but he probably wished he'd stayed in bed on 4 May 1923. He was the sole judge for the finish of a welterweight event during the afternoon, in the days before photo-finish cameras.

After what appeared to be a clear-cut result he announced his placings as first, Raceim, second, Prince Popinjay and third, Cripallen. There was an immediate outcry, but Mr Drury stood by his decision.

However, when the local newspaper, the *Brisbane Courier*, published a photograph of the finish, it was clear that Prince Popinjay had not finished second, but had actually finished *eleventh*.

The Queensland Turf Club, the premier racing body in the state, began an inquiry, and twelve days after the event, decided what the punters had known all along, that second place should be awarded to the horse Brown Cup, and that Prince Popinjay had finished out of the placings. It decreed that bets should be paid accordingly.

To rub salt into Mr Drury's wounds, the QTC fined him £25 for his mistake.

> **Brian Johnston,** as a member of the BBC's *Test Match Special* team, has livened up many cricket broadcasts with his sense of fun. Educated at Eton and New College, Oxford, he joined the Grenadier Guards during the Second World War and won the Military Cross. Brian joined BBC Outside Broadcasts in 1946 and made his name with *In Town Tonight,* broadcasting from a variety of strange sites – inside a pillar box, from the back of a horse at a circus and from a rubber dinghy while being rescued by a helicopter from the Channel.

DRESSED FOR ALL WEATHERS

In 1933, I was playing rugby football at Oxford for my college, New College and Trinity. I was not a great player, though I could run quite fast and sold a pretty nifty dummy. I was playing at centre three-quarter when I was tackled and my shorts were ripped off in the process. Luckily I was wearing a jock strap, and went to stand on the touch line while someone ran off to the pavilion to fetch another pair of shorts.

As I stood there shivering, a kind spectator offered me his mackintosh to cover my confusion.

I gratefully put it on, and watched excitedly as the ball came down the New College three-quarter line. As it reached our left wing, I couldn't resist it. I leaped on to the field and shouted: 'Outside you!'

Without looking, the left wing passed the ball swiftly to me and amidst roars from the crowd, I set off for the line. Everyone – including the referee – was laughing so much that I had no opposition and touched down triumphantly between the posts. This surely made me the first-ever player to score a try in a mackintosh, and I have not heard of anyone doing it since.

I have one small doubt in my mind about its legality. Ought I have got the referee's permission to return to the field? As it was, he was laughing so much he couldn't blow his whistle anyway.

PROUD CLAIM

Besides playing in four Tests for the 1966 British Lions Ray McLoughlin propped forty times for Ireland. His brother Feidlim wore the emerald shirt once in an international.

But nobody wore it with greater pride and it also enabled the incorrigible Feidlim to tell anyone who would listen: 'Between us my brother and I have played forty-one times for Ireland!'

Award-winning sports writer **Frank Keating** originally joined the *Guardian* Home and Foreign desk, and later returned to the paper after a ten year stint as an ITV producer in Outside Broadcasts and Special Events. In 1976 he started a daily sports column for the *Guardian*, and since then has been named both sports writer and columnist of the year. In this piece he reveals that the only worthwhile and satisfactory way for a journalist to 'cover' the Olympic Games is to:

STICK WITH THE IRISH TEAM

W hen Noel Henderson, that skilfully rumbustious centre-three-quarter of the 1950s, defined the ethos of Irish rugby football, he may as well have been speaking of all the games people play over there: 'The state of British sport is mostly serious, but never hopeless; the state of Irish sport is usually hopeless, but never serious.'

When the Irish team arrived at the Olympic Village in the high-wired, security-charged University College of Los Angeles in 1984, they found by fluke they had been assigned to quarters in H-block. By next morning, one of their number had used his ingenuity at anagrams to paint in some lettering, so H-BLOCK became SHAM-ROCK. Then they could get down to singin' songs.

The track and field events started and ended with Ireland. The marathon, the definitive spectacle that rings down the show, had the pale, frail, jug-eared boy, John Treacy, winning the silver medal. 'Sure, I had myself a very nice run out there,' he said when the world's press bombarded him with queries as to why, just a handful of days previously, he had run a semi-final and final of the 10,000 metres. But for that he would surely have won the marathon in the very kingdom of the joggers. And not only that, it was the first marathon he had ever run in his life. 'Sure, I had myself a very nice run out there.'

The field events had opened with the heats of the hammer throw. This was a special Irish day, for the guest of honour in the grandstand was Dr Pat O'Callaghan, a benign, still sturdy seventy-eight-year-old from County Cork, who had won the thing at the Los Angeles Games in 1932 with a throw of 176 ft 11 ins. He had been flown over to watch his strapping successor, Declan Hegarty, out-distance his ancient mark. Declan did not. The giant who had won the All-Ireland Welly-Throwing title at Offaly two years before, had three throws. Three times with increasing fury, he whirred and whirred around the cage, whirred and whirred and then, with an almighty aaagh! let loose the great wired balicock. Three times he demolished the wire-mesh cage.

In the grandstand in the harsh sunlight, the glint went from Dr Pat's eye. Ah, poor Declan. Down in the infield, the young Irish champion left the scaffolders to repair his damage and wandered disconsolate towards his tracksuit pile and plimsolls, trying the while to signal a 'Sorry' up there to the good old doctor. Absentmindedly, in his sorrow and annoyance, he dropped his iron hammer to the ground. It demolished his toe even more painfully than it had the aforesaid cage.

Was it in Moscow in 1980 or in Mexico that the Irish entered a diver who couldn't swim? To be sure he was a heck of a diver, but the pool he practised in at home was a tiddly thing – two little doggy-paddles and he was clutching the edge. The Olympic pool, by comparison. must have seemed as wide and dangerous as the mouth of the Shannon. So after every dive a team-mate threw him a lifebelt attached to a pole.

Was it in Montreal or in Munich that the Irish, as their dashing horsemen always are, were fancied to win a medal in the three-day event? Their best man in the cross-country was an intellectual and scholar who also had a horse to match his flair and courage in the saddle. By good fortune, he was drawn to go last of the field of thirty-seven, so he had a chance to study the lie of the land and the line that all his rivals took. His turn came at last. He tallyhoed with such nerveless vigour – that he faultlessly completed the course the wrong way round, and his penalty points ran into billions.

But, 'Sure, I had a very nice run out there.'

Which Olympics was it – and I should know

'cos I was there – that the Irish boxing second had got himself a cut eye even before the bell had gone for the first round – on account of his having swung the stool away so exuberantly as he climbed into the ring that it had swung all the way round the corner post with such a whizz that it had returned to collide clangingly with his temple!

We missed Eamon Coughlan at the 1984 Olympics. But for his injury he would surely have given either (or both) Sebastian Coe in the 1,500m or Said Aouita in the 5,000m a run for their money, as well as his great big sign-of-the-cross at the tape. In the sweltering Montreal Olympics, a good friend and colleague, Patrick Collins, was watching television in a bar one night during the qualifying rounds. The young Coughlan came down the straight, literally to cross the line in style. Two Irishmen were also at the bar as their boy in green flashed through.

They were quite beside themselves with glee. 'We've done it! He's done it! A gold for old Ireland! Drinks all round!'

Patrick felt he had to tell them it was only the qualifier. He cleared his throat and tapped one of them on the shoulder.

'It's the heat,' he pointed out.

'An' sure,' agreed Mick, 'too right, an' it must have been hot for the boy out there!'

ODDS AND SODS

Of the nineteen major rugby internationals refereed by Allan Hosie, one in particular, England versus Ireland at Twickenham in 1976, is still capable of bringing the former Scots official out in a cold sweat.

Allan was putting final touches to his preparations in the dressing room beforehand when Bob Weighill, RFU Secretary, entered with a wad of telegrams. 'Would you mind reading them out?' asked Allan, reluctant to disrupt his last minute routines.

Weighill complied ... and was stunned by the contents of one message in particular. It read: 'Would confirm your bet. £50 Ireland to win at 6-4.' It was allegedly signed 'Messrs Ladbrokes, Highenden Road, Glasgow'.

After an agonizing silence the address finally proved the giveaway so far as Allan was concerned. His club, Hillhead, is located just off Highenden Road and while relieved to identify the telegram as a prank Bob Weighill might still need convincing to this day.

Ireland scrambled their third successive Twickenham victory by a 13-12 margin with the help of a late penalty goal!

Gary Lineker, the England football captain, first played League football for Leicester in 1979. Since then, his success as a goal scorer for club and country has made him one of the best-known names in sport, and one of football's most respected ambassadors. Four goals in a match against Malaysia during the 1991 off-season lifted Gary to second place as the scorer of most goals ever for England.

SEEING THE JOKE

Anyone who plays sport at any level will have stories about their embarrassing moments on and off the pitch. I still have my leg pulled about the time I was appearing on the television programme, *A Question of Sport*, and did not recognize my old friend, the snooker player Willie Thorne, when he was the mystery guest.

But it is important to be able to look back and laugh at your mistakes and the more absurd things which happen. Cartoonists seem to have that ability, and I always admire the way they are able to extract the humour from almost any situation or subject.

Paul Johnson contributes to one or two fanzines,

the unofficial magazines which are not always kind to professional footballers. But this example, about his favourite team, Fulham, shows that you don't have to be caustic to be funny.

Bill Lothian has worked as a sports writer on the *Evening News* in his native Edinburgh since 1973. Specializing in Rugby Union, he has travelled extensively following the game, including Australia and New Zealand to cover the inaugural World Cup. As a racing tipster he has won the prestigious *Sporting Chronicle* naps championship on two occasions and has been commended in the British provincial sports journalism awards. Bill's ambition is to be picked for Scotland, at *anything*, while clinging to the hope that he is not an untalented sportsman – just a late developer!

BEATEN TO THE PUNCH

Polished speaker though he undoubtedly now is, former British Lion John Rutherford remembers with some apprehension how uncomfortable he felt about being put on the spot early in his playing days. Television interviews, in particular, would bring out the goose pimples ... until John received a tip from an old hand at broadcasting.

'Just concentrate on your opening sentence and the rest will fall into place,' John was told.

In due course an invitation was received to discuss a Scottish tour of the southern hemisphere, and John prepared for his ordeal by rehearsing the line: 'I've just returned from New Zealand where rugby is more a religion than a sport.'

No sooner had he perfected this than he was on the air. His interviewer introduced him by saying: 'With me in the studio is John Rutherford who has just returned from New Zealand where rugby is more a religion than a sport.'

MATCHLESS GAME

Fixture congestion is often such a problem for football clubs as they approach the end of the season that they end up playing three or four matches in a week.

In the York and District League, Heslington and Moor Lane Youth Club were so far behind in their season's programme that they decided to drop one match. They submitted a false 0-0 score for the 'match', and even gave the phantom referee marks out of ten for the way he handled the game.

However, word of the deceit got around, the League came to hear about it and the clubs were fined and relegated.

Barry McGuigan won the world
featherweight boxing championship in June
1985 when he defeated the champion,
Eusebio Pedroza, at Queen's Park Rangers
in London. Barry was born at Clones, just
south of the border between Northern
Ireland and the Republic, and he became
known as the 'Clones Cyclone' because of
his aggressive fighting style. At the time he
fought for the title he had won twenty-six of
his twenty-seven bouts, most of them inside
the distance. Barry made two successful
defences before losing it in the desert heat
of Las Vegas, the setting for this story.

FEELING THE BITE

When I was fighting for the title, I was
finding it increasingly difficult to make
the nine stone limit – it was tougher and
tougher, and I had to spend four to six weeks diet-
ing down to make the weight, and I would train
all the time. I can imagine what it must be like for
someone like Lester Piggot – a cigar and a cup of
coffee.

On my third defence, in Las Vegas, I lost the title
on a split decision. I just melted in the last round
in the heatwave conditions. But I had my prob-

lems before then. There was a Panamanian guy in my corner, and when I came back – I think it was after the third round, a particularly tough round for me – I was looking forward to my sixty seconds' rest. But as I sat down this guy started biting my ear. I couldn't understand what the hell he was biting my ear for. I was getting enough punishment in the ring as it was. I turned around and I asked Barney Eastwood, my Manager: 'What the hell's this guy doing?'

'Oh,' he said, 'that's to keep you alert.' Obviously he had found that this had helped with some fighters, but it shocked the living daylights out of me. It didn't do me much good either because I lost the title.

OLD HABITS DIE HARD

Scottish footballer Gary McGinnis played nine seasons with Dundee United before transferring to St Johnstone where he took on the role of team captain. During the 1990-91 season, he was looking forward to returning to United's Tannadice ground to play against his old side. However, his enthusiasm turned to embarrassment at half time when, through force of habit, he followed the United players into the home dressing room.

Ⓜ

Martyn Moxon was appointed captain of
Yorkshire County Cricket Club in 1990. He
made his debut for the county as a batsman
in 1981, and has consistently scored more
than 1,000 runs in a season. He has played
in ten Tests for England, with his highest
score 99 against New Zealand.

TAKE FIVE

O ne of the funniest things I have seen on a
cricket ground was an incident which
occurred during a John Player League
match when Yorkshire was playing Notting-
hamshire at Trent Bridge. Graham Stevenson was
batting for us, and one of the Notts fielders, Peter
Hacker, was fielding at long-off in front of a number of Yorkshire supporters. He had been receiving a lot of ribbing all afternoon from them, but
had taken it pretty well.

On one particular delivery, Graham hit the ball
in the air towards Peter who took a good catch. He
immediately turned to the crowd holding the ball
aloft, and obviously feeling pretty pleased with
himself. Unfortunately for him it was a no-ball,
but because of the noise the crowd was making he
couldn't hear his team-mates screaming from the
wicket to throw the ball in. Meanwhile the two

batsmen continued running, and by the time the confusion had been sorted out had added five to the score.

Of course we were all in stitches, but – to their credit – even some of the Notts players saw the funny side of it.

TALL TIMBERS

A young Seve Ballesteros was playing a tournament in the company of Roberto Di Vincenzo when he decided – totally out of character – to play safe at a dog leg par five.

Argentinian Di Vincenzo, in keen competition with the up and coming Spaniard, remarked: 'You know, when I was your age, Seve, I'd always hit over these trees.'

Seve bristled and reached for his No 3 wood only to see the ball clatter the timbers ...

Damage done, Di Vincenzo then added: 'But of course when I was your age, Seve, the trees were a lot smaller than they are today!'

> **Gary Oakes** and **Heather Hunt** were two of
> Britain's outstanding athletes of the 1980s.
> Heather won a bronze medal in the 4 x 100
> metres relay at the Moscow Olympics and
> two gold medals in the 100 metres and 4 x
> 100 metres relay at the 1986 Edinburgh
> Commonwealth Games. Gary also won a
> bronze medal at the Moscow Olympics in
> his event, the 400 metres hurdles. Their
> friendship on the track turned to romance,
> and they are now married with two
> children. In this story, Gary recalls the 1982
> Commonwealth Games in Brisbane.

COME ON THE CAYMANS

Heather and I have lots of shared memories
from our athletics careers, particularly of
the great occasions such as the Olympic
Games. But we particularly enjoyed the
Commonwealth gatherings – the 'friendly games'.
I remember, in Brisbane, the British team had
taken over an old London bus, sponsored by
Robinson's Barley. It had seen better days, and as
it came up the road to the stadium, it was the butt
of many an Aussie joke such as: 'Here it comes,
just like the British team, struggling to get going.'

But the spirit of the Games that year was personified by one competitor from the Cayman Islands who, like Baron Pierre de Coubertin, obviously believed taking part was more important than winning. David Bonn, the son of the Cayman team manager, competed in the 10,000 metres event, and by the time he had started the eighth lap, all of the other runners had already passed him twice.

At the finish, he was seven circuits behind all the other runners. His time for the event was a breathtaking forty-one minutes twenty-one seconds, but the large crowd still gave him an enormous ovation when he finally crossed the finishing line.

THE EVIDENCE IN BLACK AND WHITE

During a break for rain in the Test series between England and the West Indies in the 1991 season, BBC television replayed film of an old match featuring Fred Trueman, the former England fast bowler. Later, Fred was approached by someone who said he had never actually seen him bowl, but was surprised that he was much slower than he had imagined.

Fred responded immediately: 'It always looks slower in black and white.'

Sports reporters – working to tight dead-
lines – are occasionally likely to produce
copy which, on reflection, they might have
phrased differently. And the pressure
sometimes gets to the copytakers as well.

Here's a recent selection from the files
of a national newspaper, most of which –
fortunately – were picked up before publication by sharp-eyed sub editors:

RUUD HEALTH

Milan, Italy (AP) – Dutch soccer star Ruud
Gullit on Tuesday denied published
reports that he had been married for a
second time, but confirmed he's nearing
peak form.

THE LION ROARS AGAIN

British tennis, a standing joke on the international circuit for too many years, is
beginning to show signs of improvement.
Andrew Richardson, 16, a 6 ft 4 in. left han-
der from Bourne, Lincolnshire, was beaten
7-5 4-6 6-2 yesterday by Arnaud Boetsch
of France, the world number 174, but was
far from disgraced.

MEN OR MICE?

These are serious times for those who spend much of their lives trying to eek out information from Anfield.

INSIDE DOPE

Unless honours are even, one of the two sides [the Wales and Ireland Rugby teams] will at least enjoy the sweet satisfaction of winning.

UNDER THE MICROSCOPE

Ramprakash, though, remained imperceptible.

POLICE STATEMENT

Sterland's free kick was met by a lovely late run and equally fine glancing header by Speed, the ball clipping the inside of the post beyond Norman. 'You're in the wrong division' chanted a gleeful Leeds cop. It was hard to disagree.

TALKING THROUGH HIS HAIR

Referring to criticism levelled at Sulaiman, Don King said: 'It was like when the British were taxing us without representation and because they thought they were more powerful to intimidate the thirteen colonies and beat them into submission under the Pavlovian theory.'

HARD ON THE KEEPER

In the fifth minute Stephenson won a corner, took it himself and Thompson headed home from eight yards as Dibble appeared to misjudge the erection of the goalbound effort.

DADDIES SAUCE?

Leeds United continued their quest of tracking down Crystal Palace with unadulterated relish last night.

OVER THE TOP

For $3\frac{1}{2}$ years, Steffi Graf was the best. Sometimes she was even better than that.

LAGER LOUT

Phil Pugh, warned in the first half after a midfield pub brawl, was sent off by referee Les Peard for a dangerous tackle on full-back, Mark Yendle.

DEATH RATTLE

The US Bobsled and Skeleton Federation has four months to turn over financial documents to auditors or face de-certification as a national governing body.

NEVER TOO LATE

Scotland rugby flanker Finlay Calder, has told how he took exception to some disparaging comments made by an All Black during a quarter-final tie in the 1987 World Cup.

Calder vowed revenge and the chance came on a muddy pitch during the 1988 Sydney Sevens. Chasing a kick ahead Calder carried through and tackled the All Black after the ball had been played.

In response to a cry of 'Here, that was late', he replied: 'Yep – a year late.'

BIT THICK (1)

In respect of the past few years, we're definitely more concrete, said Sampdoria playmaker, Roberto Mancini.

BIT THICK (2)

The former Great Britain sweeper, Moira MacLeod, was a rock in Scotland's defence, with Janet Nimmo and the captain Margery Coutts also solid.

OFF THE TOP OF THE HEAD

But Norwich's reply was emphatic, Power putting on a head from close range after thirteen minutes when Phillips turned back across goal a cross from Gordon.

ANY EXCUSE

Polish star Grzegorz Filipowski has a broken leg and has pulled out of next week's world figure skating championships in Munich.

INFLATION BEGINS TO BITE

Toshack's contract, worth a reported 270 million pesetas (pounds 1.5), ties him to the Basque club until 1996.

VERY TRUE

Bridgend 9 Newbridge 4. The quest for two pints has become the over-riding factor in the inaugural season of the Heineken League.

TAKE COVER

Wickramasinghe produced a succession of lofted drives and poles which conveniently fell into the open spaces.

POST-SURGERY

He showed an old head on tender shoulders as he raced through on to Neil Webb's pass.

ON SONG

Tait is running back into the kind of form that has made him into one of the outstanding concerts to the professional game from north of the border.

Paul Parker has been Sussex county cricket captain since 1988, and has played for England at Test level. He has scored 1,000 runs in a season on eight occasions, and 40 first-class centuries. He is a Cambridge Blue at cricket, and was selected for the Varsity rugby match in 1977, but had to withdraw through injury.

A CLOSE ENCOUNTER

At international level there is increasing concern over the standard of sportsmanship. Fortunately, in county cricket this is not a problem, and there are very few instances of cheating and accusations of cheating.

Early in my career, I was involved in one dubious incident. In 1977, Somerset were entertaining Sussex in a mid-season championship match at Taunton. The wicket was green and conditions were perfect for swing and seam bowling. Somerset had won the toss and had elected to field. Their opening attack of Joel Garner and Ian Botham had soon reduced Sussex to 44 for 5 when I arrived at the crease. I was facing the 6'8" West Indian Garner, and the first ball I received was on a good length on the off stump. It reared past my

nose and the keeper, Derek Taylor, took the ball on
the rise at head height.

The captain of Somerset at that stage was a bald-
ing Yorkshireman, Brian Close, who was standing
in his customary position of short leg. Just before
Garner set off to deliver his second delivery to me,
Close stood up at short leg and brought proceed-
ings to an abrupt halt.

'Hold it, Joel!' echoed round the ground.

Close surveyed his field and made several
strategic alterations, and suffice to say I was sur-
rounded: leg-slip, short-leg, silly-mid-on and silly-
mid-off, cover and an array of slip fielders.
Garner's next delivery was the same length as his
first , but slightly straighter. The ball thudded into
my chest and high into the air in the direction of
the leg-slip. Eleven Somerset men shouted 'Catch
it!' The ball evaded leg-slip and went down to the
vacant fine leg boundary for four leg byes – or so I
thought. As I was running up the wicket rubbing
the bruised area, I saw the umpire, John Langridge
(the former Sussex batsman!) signalling four runs.
I was puzzled, but naturally happy about this as it
meant that I was off the mark.

Later on, when I was standing at the non-strik-
er's end, John Langridge leaned towards me and
enquired: 'You didn't hit that, Paul, did you?'

'No, John, I didn't get anywhere near it.'

'I didn't think so. They tried to cheat you out, so
I thought I'd give you four for it anyway.'

John Parrott won the Embassy World Snooker Championship in 1991, defeating Steve Davis in the semi-finals and Jimmy White in the final at the Crucible in Sheffield. His secret ambition is to own the winning horse in the Champion Hurdle at Cheltenham.

A DAY IN THE LIFE ...

I have always had the luxury of being driven to my matches over the years, either by my manager Phil Miller, or by my close friend, Tony Shirley. When Phil took me under his wing, I wasn't old enough to drive anyway.

I can remember vividly when the travel wasn't quite so exotic as driving in my current BMW, and when the hours were even more unsociable than they can be today.

One Saturday, I think in 1981, I had to play in a junior tournament at a golf club, of all places, near Swindon. To get there for a 9am start, Phil had to pick me up some five hours earlier from my home in Liverpool.

In those days, Phil drove a T-registered Ford Escort, and we were soon heading along the M6 for the West Country. However, between

Knutsford and Keele services, the car spluttered to a halt.

Now, I'm not mechanically minded one bit so it was up to Phil to get out of the car and try to get it going again. Unfortunately it was raining cats and dogs, and as he fiddled with bits and pieces under the bonnet, the HGVs going by drenched him with spray from head to foot.

I couldn't stop laughing, which didn't go down very well with him, and his language was somewhat coarse. Eventually the engine burst into life again and we were able to resume our journey after a delay of about twenty minutes.

We weren't late for my first match, and while I can't remember the name of my opponent, it was all over in twenty-five minutes. I lost 2-0.

Even though Phil was still feeling just a little damp, there was no point in hanging around so we headed back home to finish off a nine hour return journey for just twenty-five minutes of snooker – and there wasn't even a radio in the car to break the boredom.

OFF COURSE

Horse racing has provided some strange results over the years, but one of the most bizarre was recorded at Wexford in Ireland in March 1988. The event was the three-mile Rathnure Handicap in which almost all the thirteen runners lost their way.

During the first circuit the leading horse, Lady Daffydown, took the rest of the field around the wrong side of a marker. Jockey Pat O'Donnell on Derry Gowan realized what had happened, and returned to take the correct course. The diversion meant that Derry Gowan came in last of the ten finishers. However, after a lengthy stewards' inquiry during which officials viewed a poor quality video film of the race, the first nine horses were disqualified. Derry Gowan, the last horse to finish, was placed first.

Later, a second video of the race turned up. That clearly showed that another horse, Mullakhea, which had passed the finishing post in sixth place, had clearly rounded the course marker on the correct side. The horse's connections appealed to the Irish National Hunt Committee, and it agreed to hear the new evidence. The Committee met six days after the race had been run.

The appeal was upheld, and so the horse which had finished sixth was placed first. Following on from that, the horse which had finished last and first, was placed second.

Not only jockeys sometimes lose their way!

>
> **Fred Perry** was the last British Men's
> Wimbledon champion, taking the title three
> years in a row from 1934-6. He also helped
> Britain to four successive Davis Cup
> victories. Soon after, he turned professional
> and spent much of his time touring the
> American circuit. After he was lost to the
> amateur game, Britain lost the Davis Cup
> and has never won it since.

AHEAD OF HIS TIME

After I turned professional, and we were still persona non grata in anywhere but America, I was playing in an exhibition match in Connecticut in, I think, 1938 when the knee of my long trousers split. I didn't have another pair with me, but we had to do something about it, and it was decided the best thing was just to cut the legs off.

Unfortunately the only scissors available were a pair of ladies' cuticle scissors. The lady who owned them cut the legs off for me, just above the knee, making them into a pair of longish shorts. Of course, the legs didn't match, and they had wavy lines all round the bottoms. As we were not normally allowed to wear anything but long trousers to play tennis, this was my first effort in shorts – and I think the only time – and it lasted about one and a half sets.

So it was all rather embarrassing to think that my only appearance in what passes for normal wear today, was in a pair of bermuda-style shorts with serrated edges round the bottoms.

'OH NO HE ISN'T!'

The Middlesex and England cricketer, Denis Compton, once recalled an incident during the New Zealand tour of England in 1949 when the day's play often started at 11.30. Compton was due to bat in the second Test at the Oval, but was held up by traffic at Marble Arch shortly after 11 o'clock. A motorist in the next car was listening to the match on his car radio when he noticed Compton beside him.

'Shouldn't you be at the Oval?'

'Yes,' said Compton. 'I'm on my way now.'

'But you should be there,' said the driver, as he turned up the car radio. 'It's an 11 o'clock start.'

To the cricketer's horror, he heard the commentator say: 'Denis Compton is the next batsman, and he will be coming down the steps any moment now.'

David Rhys Jones is the BBC's principal bowls commentator, and has partnered world bowls champion, David Bryant, since 1965. He has shared ten of David Bryant's twenty-six national titles.

A DROP IN THE OCEAN

When David Bryant won the Commonwealth Games singles title for the second time in 1970, the Clevedon town council debated what they should do to mark his achievement.

'He's a keen fisherman,' said one councillor, who knew that David spent hours at the end of the town's Victorian pier, dangling a line in the hope of a catch.

So, with due ceremony, the council arranged for David to receive 'The Freedom of the Pier', so that he could be excused the three (old) pence levy.

David was naturally touched by the gesture – but, before he could take advantage of it ... the pier had fallen into the sea.

Twenty years later, the pier is still under reconstruction, and David, still the world champion, is waiting to take advantage of his honour.

'Hope you don't mind – I ran out of dental floss this morning'

A leading Scottish rugby player, competing in the exotic Hong Kong Sevens, was asked by an Arab contemporary at a social gathering: 'Do you get stoned for adultery in Scotland?'

The reply stopped the Arab in his tracks. 'No – but I find a couple of gin and tonics do help me to relax.'

Andy Ripley was one of England's most exciting rugby players during the 1970s and was England's captain twenty-five times. He also played for the British Lions and the Barbarians.

HEADING FOR TROUBLE

Rugby can be a tough game, and I've known players suffer some strange injuries. There was one that happened to a wing forward called Brian Chorley, who played for Old Windsorians in the early 1970s.

He was involved in a collision with an opposition player during a match against Camberley. His head struck the opponent's face so heavily that he had to have a number of stitches, and the other player lost three teeth.

When Brian Chorley had his stitches removed, he still had a lump. One day, when scratching his head over a problem, he dislodged a tooth from his scalp.

BOUNCED CZECH

Footballers sent off for foul play some-times complain about the harshness of the referee's decision. Stanislav Griga, a Czech playing in the Netherlands, has stronger grounds than most for complaining about the referee's decision in a match in March 1991 – he was sent off because of his nationality.

Stanislav was playing for Feyenoord of Rotterdam in the Dutch league, and in a match against Willem II Tilburg he lined up with nine Dutch players and a Hungarian for the start of the match. However, in the sixty-seventh minute, former Norwich City player, Mark Farrington, replaced one of the Dutch players. This was in breach of the Dutch Football Association's rules that only two non-national players can be fielded at any one time.

Shortly afterwards, the referee realized what had happened, and Griga was sent from the field – for no greater offence than the fact that he was a Czech, and happened to be standing nearby.

Feyenoord was not allowed to play another substitute, and finished the match with ten men. To increase their agony, the Rotterdam side lost 1-0.

Former primary school headteacher **Andy Roxburgh** has been the Scottish Football Association's national coach since 1986, and took his team to the World Cup finals in Italy in 1990. He has had a long career in football, as a professional player with Falkirk, Partick Thistle and Clydebank, as a coach with Clydebank, and as coach of Scotland's under-age teams from 1975.

THE JUNKET

When people in public life go on a business trip to some glamorous destination, the media sometimes describe the excursion as a junket. This is a popular American term which refers to a trip made for pleasure which is paid for by public funds. The suggestion is that it is really a vacation at someone else's expense.

Before the last World Cup in Italy, Ernie Walker, the Scottish Football Association General Secretary at the time, and I were on a 'grand tour' in order to assess facilities and to make provisional arrangements for our team's accommodation. Early one morning – 6.30 am to be precise – we were waiting in Bologna railway station. E.W. was trying to consume a lukewarm cup of cappucino and a two-day old roll filled with hard, less-than-appetising parma ham. A cold wind blew around our legs, and the dust irritated our tired, blood-shot eyes. Ernie turned to me and asked in a pathetic tone: 'Is this a junket?' It was a rhetorical question!

Later that day, we arrived in Udine in the north-east of Italy. I took E.W. to meet an old friend of mine, football fan and celebrated artist, Celiberti. The great man's home was also his studio and the ambience and decor were sumptuous. On the wall of the lounge hung original paintings and draw-ings by Salvador Dali, Picasso and other world-famous artists. Ernie stood there in these fabulous surroundings with a glass of champagne in one hand and a cigar in the other. He looked at me and, fourteen hours after the Bologna experience, he enthusiastically declared: 'Now this *is* a junket!'

When we returned to Italy for the World Championship in June 1990, the event had so many frustrations and disappointments from Scotland's point of view that nobody could possi-bly describe it as a junket. Who knows, maybe in the United States in 1994, we shall experience the full pleasure of the term, à la Celiberti!

BLOOD RELATION

When light heavyweight boxer Steve McCarthy stepped into the ring for a bout against Tony Wilson in Southampton in

1989, he soon discovered that Wilson's mother was actually a more formidable opponent.

McCarthy soon gained the upper hand in the fight, scoring an early knockdown against his opponent. In the third round Tony Wilson had been backed into a corner and was taking heavy punishment. This proved too much for his mother, Minna Wilson, who was watching the fight. She leapt into the ring, took off one of her high-heeled shoes and began beating McCarthy around the head with it.

She was finally pulled away, leaving a bemused and bleeding McCarthy to ponder on the unexpected dangers of the fight game. His response was to refuse to carry on with the bout on the grounds that he had suffered a cut to the head from Mrs Wilson's shoe.

He was then disqualified for not continuing, and Wilson was declared the winner – a decision which was later upheld by the British Boxing Board of Control. However, to settle the matter properly in the ring, the two fighters were ordered to meet again.

In the interests of a fair fight – and Steve McCarthy's safety – Mrs Wilson was banned from attending the rematch.

Tessa Sanderson has represented Britain in the javelin event since 1973, and has won one Olympic Games and three Common-wealth Games gold medals. She has won a string of other world and European titles, and in 1985 became an MBE in recognition of her services to sport. She is currently training for the 1992 Olympics, and if selected would make a record fifth Olympic Games appearance.

TWO RIGHT FEET

Just before the Los Angeles Olympics in 1984, I went to Hungary for a special training session with Miklos Memeth. On the first morning, when everyone was getting ready to throw, I went to put on my special javelin boots. Would you believe it, I discovered I had brought two right feet out with me. The worst of it was that I couldn't get replacements and I was out there for ten days.

I just had to make the best of it, and wear them for the whole time while we were training. Of course, nobody had any sympathy for me, and they were all laughing because they kept seeing me wandering around wearing two right javelin shoes, with both my toes at funny angles. No one has ever let me forget that since then.

E IS FOR ...

Alun Lewis, the Cambridge scrum half, was a newcomer to the Welsh rugby squad when, feeding a practice scrummage, he was responsible for calling a code to activate back row moves.

Any word beginning with the letter E would indicate a pick up by Trevor Evans. Lewis's intellectual capacity did not endear him to some of the more artisan members of the pack, however. The first word which entered his mind was 'enigma', not one that commands a regular place in the vocabulary of the average front rower. The scrum buckled with laughter and as the forwards pulled themselves together Lewis was put in his place.

'What's wrong with eggs ... bloody eggs next time!' snarled hooker Bobby Windsor.

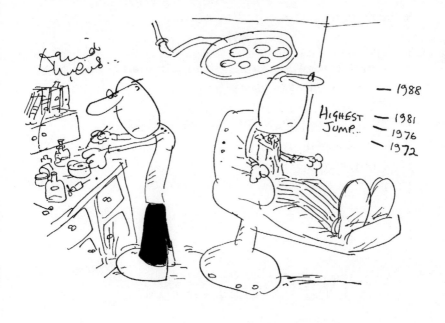

OH REALLY?

Tony O'Reilly, the former Ireland rugby three-quarter who has risen to become Number One in the giant Heinz conglomerate, was recalled in 1970 to win his twenty-ninth cap for Ireland at Twickenham aged thirty-four, seven years after his previous international appearance.

One Irish newspaper took the view that this was turning back the clock a bit too much and struck the headline: 'Heinz Meanz Haz Beanz'.

> ⓜ
>
> **Chris Tavaré** is a tall right-handed batsman
> who has played more than thirty times for
> England, and has toured Australia, New
> Zealand, Pakistan and India and Sri Lanka.
> Although he began his cricket career with
> Kent, he now plays for Somerset and has
> been captain for the past two seasons.

AN UNFORGETTABLE SLIP

What could have been my most embarrassing moment in sport turned into a
moment of great triumph. But that
doesn't stop people constantly reminding me of it.

On the tour of Australia in 1982/83, we went to
Melbourne for the Fourth Test 2-0 down in the
series with two matches left. It was vital to win if
we were to have a chance of retaining the Ashes,
that most coveted of cricket trophies.

Australia needed 292 to win in their second
innings, but had slumped to 218 for 9 when Jeff
Thomson joined Allan Border. It looked a formali-
ty for us, but the last pair started to add runs
slowly until they needed just four to win.

Ian Botham bowled to Thomson, and the ball
was edged to second slip where I was fielding.

I've got it... No. I haven't.

The ball slipped from my grasp, looping over my head. The consequences would be disastrous, the match and the Ashes lost, and shame for evermore – the man who dropped Jeff Thomson.

Yet my saviour was at hand, and Geoff Miller ran round from first slip to take the catch, and we were triumphant. I think I even managed a smile!

Some years later autograph collectors still ask me to sign a certain photograph showing Geoff Miller taking the famous catch with me looking on rather alarmed. I will never be allowed to forget that moment.

FOREIGN FIELDS

A French referee was on an exchange trip to Glasgow but the visit was marred when he had cause to send a player off for misconduct. The miscreant was not in the least remorseful though and, before retiring for first use of the soap, gave vent to his feelings in a sudden gush of expletives.

Whereupon the French official, who spoke limited English, was momentarily touched with pity before standing firm. 'Non,' he insisted, wagging an admonishing finger in the direction of the pavilion. 'Eet eez too late now for your apologeez'.

David Wilkie won Britain's first Olympic gold medal in the swimming pool since 1908 when he took the 200 metres breaststroke title in Montreal in 1976. He was the holder of five world records, thirty British, sixteen European and twenty-three Commonwealth records. He also holds three world records in masters swimming events.

CATCH THE COACH

Back in 1973 I accepted a scholarship to the University of Miami to study marine biology. This scholarship was given to me because of my swimming ability, and for the next four years I was expected to represent the university in various collegiate swim meets all over the United States.

I will never forget one particular meet, not because I won, but because that day I learnt something about my coach – something I wished I never knew.

The meet was against the University of Florida, a powerhouse in American swimming and a university that had been Miami's great rival for many years. In fact we had never actually beaten them.

A crowd of some 3,000 turned up on the day to watch some of the best swimmers in the world battle it out for their universities. With the lead changing many times, the result had come down to the last relay – a 4 by 100 medley event.

The atmosphere by now was electric, with 3,000 students baying for Florida's blood, and demanding a victory from us. The pressure was on. After the backstroke leg, we were down, but the lead was regained on the next leg, the breaststroke. On the butterfly it was neck and neck.

Then on the last leg the swimmers entered the water together. Swimmers of both teams were now lining the pool shouting encouragement, and the crowd had risen in anticipation. Twenty-five metres to go and it was still neck and neck.

With ten metres to go, the Florida swimmer was tiring. Sensing this, our man powered home for victory. Miami had won for the first time in history, and the whole place went wild. We looked around for our coach to give him the celebratory dip, and knowing that, I suppose we didn't think it strange at the time that he was heading for the exit.

Eventually he was caught, and summarily dispatched into the depths of the University of Miami's swimming pool. He went up and down three times gasping and fighting for air. On the fourth time it became abundantly clear that he was not joking – the man I had entrusted to guide me to Olympic gold could not swim.

Three years later, he did take me on to win an Olympic gold medal. Six months before the event, he predicted to within 0.11 of a second my winning time. Not bad for a non-swimmer.

EXCUSE ME

One of the most original reasons ever put forward for pulling out of a rugby match was given on political grounds. Dominic Addington, an Aberdeen University student, withdrew from a Scottish students team match in the mid-80s because the fixture clashed with his maiden speech in the House of Lords where he is known as Baron Addington.

Equally genuine, but no less unusual, was a call-off 'excuse' provide by Carnoustie player Ian Lamont. A diver employed in the North Sea oil industry, Ian called his team secretary one Friday evening to explain that a submarine had collided with a rig which meant he had to work a spot of overtime repairing the damage instead of playing rugby.

Barrie Williams achieved national fame in 1989 as the articulate manager of the non-Football League side, Sutton United, which beat First Division team, Coventry City 2-1 in the third round of the FA Cup. The former high school English teacher was often known to quote Shakespeare, Kipling and the Venerable Bede in his programme notes. He has moved on from Sutton United to work for a sports insurance company, and is now also manager of the England women's football team.

LAST LAUGH FOR THE JOKER

Every football dressing room has its practical joker. Not for him the off-the-cuff witticism, not for him the telling of a previously heard joke; his is a preconceived, well thought-out, deliberate action. He is good, his successes numerous, yet never malicious.

Take the Thursday night during training at Sutton United when the resident joker secreted some pornographic magazines in the bags of those players whose kit would later be washed by their wives or mothers. Some of the subsequent stories after 'The Sting' were memorable: the report of bag, kit – and magazine – being hurled out of the fourth floor window of a flat; others of usually placid spouses tearing the offending publications into shreds and flushing them down the toilet; and of mothers, in hurt tones, demanding explanations of their innocent sons.

Then, after team-mates began to receive free membership to the Surrey Ramblers Guild, and visits from insurance company representatives, it was decided that something should be done about the Joker.

The club always had close relations with the local police, and PCs, sergeant and inspector were often welcome visitors for match duty, to discuss cup tie arrangements and for charity events. Therefore, it was decided to seek 'friendly' police assistance for our retribution.

The Thursday night training session began on the pitch at 7pm, with the players arriving at 6.30. And so it was that for one such evening, the police agreed to turn up in a squad car at 6.45pm, siren blaring and lights flashing – the plan requiring them to be three-handed, correctly uniformed and in haste.

They were to rush into the dressing room, search out the Joker and advise him, in full view of his onlooking team-mates, of his rights. He was to be advised that he had been recognized and named as the person seen 'showing off' in a High Street toilet.

They would then march him off, handcuffed if

possible, to the car where, sirens blaring once more, he would be taken to the station and held in a cell for ten minutes.

That, anyway, was the plan. But fate intervened in the form of fog. The team was due to play a match two days before the pay-back but, as dense fog descended, the game was postponed and rescheduled for that particular Thursday.

It was only at noon on the day that it was realized that at 6.45pm the Joker – who also just happened to be a most gifted and prolific goalscorer – would be whisked off to a police cell just before the start of the match, unless the police could be contacted.

Panic soon became terror because none of the police participants were on duty until later in the day. Fortunately, not long after, the sergeant popped in to check last-minute details.

And so the great attempt at table-turning was aborted – never to be enacted – as the plan was revealed to the Joker the next day by a person unknown.

The story does not quite finish there. I, as manager, found comfort from smoking my pipe during games, but was quite often known to lose it afterwards. Such was the case after this rearranged match.

I shall always wonder – when I discovered it on my desk the next day and lit it in relief at its finding – who put the Sanilav toilet cleaner in it, thereby rendering my favourite briar to the rack of pain!

Barrie Williams recounts a further story from his days with Sutton United:
For several seasons, we had in the Sutton line-up a speedy and likeable forward called Francis Awaritefe (pronounced our-wa-ra-tee-fee). He could be depended on to rise to the big occasion, and made a notable contribution in our third round FA Cup match in 1988 when we drew 1-1 at home against the leading second division side, Middlesborough.

However, Francis ran foul of the referee on a number of occasions for his hard running and over-enthusiastic approach to the game. Once, he was called over by the referee after a stern tackle which sent the opposition player crashing. The official immediately reached for his notebook.

'Right then, what's your name?' he demanded to know.

'Francis Awaritefe, Sir.'

The referee reflected for just a moment, put away his book, and said: 'Okay, son. Just don't do it again.'

QUICK RECOVERY

The former BBC sports commentator, John Snagge, liked to tell the story about the radio presenter, reading out the cricket scores...

'Yorkshire 232 all out, Hutton ill – I'm sorry, Hutton, one hundred and eleven.'

Welshman **Ian Woosnam** confirmed his position as the world's number one golfer when he won the 1991 US Masters title at Augusta, Georgia. Previously he was runner-up in the US Open in 1989, and has been a member of the European Ryder Cup team since 1983. In this piece he recalls how, after turning professional in 1976 and early on in his career, he could not always concentrate entirely on his golf when preparing for an important event:

MY GOLF VW

I had borrowed my father's old Volkswagen caravanette for the tour. It was white, going off-white, so I painted it blue to make it look a bit more respectable. It became a real home from home as we travelled around. We slept in it, dried our clothes in it, and ate our rather monotonous fare of crisps, soup and endless tins of baked beans in it.

I didn't have much trouble getting a good night's rest in the van, but moving around in it presented more problems. I just prayed it wouldn't break down because I had no money for repairs. It took me more than three days to drive to Milan, but once there, the old banger began to splutter and choke and slowed down to an embarrassing ten miles an hour crawl, its top speed.

I hawked it from one garage to another, fearing that the engine had broken up. How on earth was I going to find several hundred quid for a new one? No one seemed to be able to diagnose the trouble till at last I found a Volkswagen dealer.

He fixed it in moments – a tube had come off the carburettor, and once it was back on, the VW ran like a bird. In spite of this preparation, I came ninth in the Italian Open, so at least I had enough money for the petrol home

---

HUMPTY HAKA

Scotland's rugby team, touring New Zealand in 1990, had no intention of being intimidated or psyched out by the All Blacks immediately before the Test matches.

To the extent that when the world champions performed their legendary haka war dance immediately before kick off, the Scots launched their own counter offensive. 'We linked arms,' recalls centre threequarter Scott Hastings,'and recited the words of the Humpty Dumpty nursery rhyme to the rhythm of the haka.'

AFTERWORD
by Gyles Brandreth
Chairman, National Playing Fields Association

The royalties of this book are going to help the work of the National Playing Fields Association (NPFA) – the national trust of recreational space.

This book has been made possible through the support of many of our leading sportspeople, broadcasters and cartoonists. Because of their generosity, all royalties will be used for the important work the National Playing Fields Association is currently undertaking – fighting the loss of playing fields throughout the United Kingdom and working to improve sport, play and playground facilities for young people, especially those with disabilities.

Sixty-six years ago the NPFA was established with a simple mandate: every child has the right to play. Nothing could be simpler. Yet our society is losing sight of this fundamental idea.

The NPFA has not done so, and today it is one of the most effective voices in the campaign for better play provision. It is not a fashionable cause. Nor, on the surface, is it an emotional cause. It is a cause concerned with the bed-rock on which our society is founded.

We live in a world designed and built for adults by adults. Children must learn to live in this world too. It is the world in which they have to grow. A vital part of that growing-up process is play. For children, play is not trivial or unimportant. It helps them to learn, to solve problems, and to work together. It is in their play that children learn about life and about living – their preparation for the future. Sports and games stimulate optimum growth and development, encourage team spirit and prepare children for the competitive environment. Without such opportunities, the deprived child develops into the deprived adult.

A concern for how children play and grow and develop is a concern for the future and the shape our society will take. The NPFA believes that we are failing our children, ourselves and our future in this key area. But it is still not too late, though the call for action grows more urgent.

We call our world 'the developed world'. How do children see it? They see high-rise flats, estates with postage-stamp sized gardens, signs saying 'Keep off the Grass' and 'No Ball Games Here'. Plans for new residential developments must include provisions for adequate parking space, but there is no similar requirement for play space. And it is not only to children that the environment has become alien, almost hostile, but to adults as well. We have separated children from adults in their work, their education and their leisure.

We are destroying their play world. We are placing our children at risk, and in doing so we place our own future at risk. The simple needs are those most quickly forgotten.

The Real Needs

In providing real play opportunities we can no longer salve our consciences by giving expensive toys and play equipment. Just to provide swings and roundabouts is only scratching at the surface of children's real needs. It is not just a question of play space and equipment. Children need:

to be creative

to be stimulated and challenged

to be involved in all aspects of life

otherwise they will seek their excitement in other ways.

Most of all the NPFA believes children need people. Children need the care and involvement of adults in their play. This means nothing less than a total change of attitudes. Bringing children – and their play – into the centre of our lives and thinking.

When we plan for children we plan for our future. The NPFA believes this means fighting for children:

to give them space

to give them time to play

to involve people in their play.

Above all else, the NPFA is fighting for the child's right to play. It means making the right choices in allocating our national resources. Play is cost effective because:

it saves repairing children's bodies and minds

it saves by reducing delinquency, violence and vandalism

it saves by reducing stress in families.

That is what the NPFA's campaign for children's play is about. It is the only organization with the potential to fight effectively for children's play. We urgently need your help and support:

to create a greater understanding of the value of play to children

to persuade both public and private sectors of their responsibilities to children

to improve the quantity and the quality of play opportunities for children

to support means of involving adults in the play – and therefore the lives – of children.

If you would like to know more about the charity and its work, write to me for further imformation:

Gyles Brandreth
The National Playing Fields Association
25 Ovington Square
London SW3 1LQ
Telephone: 071-584 6445

Every Child Deserves a Place to Play